Medicare's New Hospital Payment System

MEDICARE'S NEW HOSPITAL PAYMENT SYSTEM
Is It Working?

LOUISE B. RUSSELL

THE BROOKINGS INSTITUTION
WASHINGTON, D.C.

Library of Congress Cataloging-in-Publication Data
Russell, Louise B.
  Medicare's new hospital payment system : is it working? / Louise
B. Russell.
      p.   cm.
  Includes bibliographical references.
  ISBN 0-8157-7624-1 (alk. paper)   ISBN 0-8157-7623-3 (pbk. : alk. paper)
  1. Medicare.   2. Hospitals—United States—Prospective payment—
Evaluation.   I. Brookings Institution.   II. Title.
HD7102.U4R865   1989
368.4'26'0140973—dc20   89-22079
                                                                       CIP

9   8   7   6   5   4   3   2   1

The paper used in this publication meets the minimum requirements
of the American National Standard for Information Sciences—Per-
manence of Paper for Printed Library Materials, ANSI Z39.48-1984.

Typeset in Linotron Sabon
Composition by Graphic Composition, Inc.
Athens, Georgia
Printing by R.R. Donnelley and Sons, Co.
Harrisonburg, Virginia
Book Design by Ken Sabol
Cover by Stephen Kraft

FOREWORD

—————

IN 1983, with projected spending outrunning revenues, medicare introduced a new way of paying hospitals, replacing reimbursement of actual costs with a system of prospective rates based on the patient's diagnosis. The goal was to slow the relentless growth in the program's expenditures for hospital care, which had ballooned from $5 billion in 1970 to $37 billion in 1982. Hospitals were expected to react to the fixed payment system by becoming more efficient in providing inpatient care and making greater use of alternative kinds of care.

Enough time has now elapsed to assess the performance of the new system on both financial savings and the quality of care. Decisions will be made over the next year or two that will be critical in determining the long-term course of prospective payment and of the medicare program.

In this book Louise B. Russell offers an evaluation of the new payment system. She finds that prospective payment has accomplished its primary goal by achieving substantial savings, without shifting costs to other payers. Reliable data about changes in the quality of care are hard to come by, but the available evidence does not show any clear-cut deterioration in quality. The issue is a crucial one, however, and she recommends that surveillance be continued and improved. The author concludes that prospective payment has provided a valuable framework for debate over how much the nation will pay for health care for the elderly and for what services.

Louise B. Russell is research professor of economics in the Institute for Health, Health Care Policy, and Aging Research at Rutgers University, and professor in the Department of Economics; she was a senior fellow at the Brookings Institution until 1987. Of the many people who gave advice and assistance with the research, she is especially grateful to Julian H. Pettengill, Stephen H. Long, and Steven H. Sheingold for providing comments and information in the course of the study. The draft manuscript benefited from careful reviews by Paul B. Ginsburg, Julian H. Pettengill, Alice M. Rivlin, Charles L. Schultze, and an anonymous reviewer.

Carrie Lynn Manning, co-author of the section on Peer Review Organizations in chapter 4, also provided research assistance for most other sections of the study. The author thanks her for handling many difficult tasks superbly, including the computation of medicare's savings from prospective payment. Mary Skinner provided research assistance during the early stages of the study.

Jeanette Morrison edited the manuscript, Anna M. Nekoranec and Victor M. Alfaro checked it for factual accuracy, Susan L. Woollen provided editorial assistance, and Florence Robinson prepared the index.

This study was funded in part by The Colorado Trust. The views expressed are the author's and should not be attributed to the officers, trustees, or staff members of the Brookings Institution, to Rutgers University, to The Colorado Trust, or to any of those who were consulted or who commented on the manuscript.

BRUCE K. MAC LAURY
President

July 1989
Washington, D.C.

CONTENTS

Tables

Figures

Medicare's New Hospital Payment System

CHAPTER ONE

Introduction

IN 1983 Congress dramatically changed the way medicare pays for hospital care for its elderly and disabled beneficiaries. Until then, hospitals had been paid the actual costs incurred in treating these patients and could be sure that, with occasional exceptions, their costs would be covered in full. Under the new, "prospective" payment system, medicare pays a fixed rate, set in advance, for a patient's hospital stay. If costs are less than the rate, the hospital keeps the profit; if they are more, it must absorb the loss.

The new payment system has already had important effects on hospitals and the medical sector. Some observers have hailed it as a successful way to control the spiraling expenditures of the medicare program, while others have criticized it as arbitrary and a threat to the health of the elderly because it may encourage the omission of necessary services. The purpose of this book is to offer a comprehensive assessment of the evidence about prospective payment and to suggest where on the spectrum between those two extremes the new system belongs.

Legislative History

Medicare is the federal program that helps pay the hospital and doctors' bills of the elderly, the disabled, and those with end-stage kidney disease. Like social security, the hospital part of the program (Part A) is financed by a tax on wages paid in equal parts by employers and employees. The tax revenues are held in a special fund, the Hospital Insurance Trust Fund, and paid out as bills are presented. A second fund, the Supplementary Medical Insurance Trust Fund, collects the premium payments and general tax revenues that pay for doctors' bills and related services (Part B).

From 1966, when the program began, until 1982 hospitals were paid their costs. Backed by such a generous system of payment, hospitals' expenditures grew rapidly year after year, at rates well over inflation, as they expanded their services and brought in new employees and equipment to produce those services.[1] Outlays under the program quickly exceeded the original projections: expenditures for hospital care reached $37 billion by 1982, up from $5 billion in 1970.[2] Although a number of minor modifications were made in this cost-based system of reimbursement, it was still largely intact in 1982.

By then, however, the situation had reached crisis point. The trustees of the Hospital Insurance Trust Fund projected that the fund would run out of money by the end of the decade, perhaps as early as 1987, only five years away.[3] At the same time, the social security program was also in serious financial trouble, and a distinguished advisory commission was convened to come up with solutions. Its deliberations took place amid strong feelings of urgency, heightened by the fact that the federal government as a whole was running a huge deficit.

In what was later described by one congressman as "an almost desperate act,"[4] Congress approved legislation in August 1982 setting limits on medicare's reimbursement of hospital costs for the next three fiscal years, and requiring the secretary of health and human services, in consultation with the committees on Finance and Ways and Means, to submit a plan for permanent payment reform by the end of the year. The limits were part of the Tax Equity and Fiscal Responsibility Act of 1982, a mammoth budget bill aimed at reducing the federal deficit and passed under the pressures created by that deficit. During consideration of the bill, the discussion made it clear that many congressmen expected the reimbursement limits to be replaced by some form of prospective payment, a method in which rates of payment are set in advance of the period to which they apply.[5]

A plan was duly submitted in late December. It proposed that prospective rates be set for 467 diagnosis-related groups—groups of patients with similar medical conditions. Developed from the costs historically associated with treatment for each condition, the rates for these groups would cover all hospital operating costs, but the costs of capital and medical education would continue to be paid separately. The rates would be adjusted for the wage level in each labor market and would be increased each year to reflect, in the degree considered appropriate by the secretary, inflation, productivity in the industry, and the need to spend on new technology. Together with the deductible and copayment amounts already required of beneficiaries, the rates would constitute payment in full. Hospitals could keep any profits, but would also have to shoulder any losses.[6]

The plan was coupled with the changes in social security recommended by the advisory commission and moved rapidly through Congress. The formal bill embodying the plan was submitted on February 23, 1983. By March 25 both houses of Congress had agreed on a final bill and sent it on to the president. While accepting the plan's main features, Congress included several important changes designed to make it more equitable in its effects on hospitals. Instead of a single set of national rates, rates were to be set separately for urban and rural hospitals. A three-year phase-in period was introduced during which urban and rural rates would also be established for each of the nine census regions in the country, and payment would be based on a blend of the individual hospital's costs, the regional rates, and the national rates. Finally, exemptions were permitted to allow states with their own rate-setting programs to continue to operate them.[7]

The Social Security Amendments of 1983, containing the prospective payment plan, were signed into law on April 20, 1983.[8] Prospective payment was slated to go into effect on October 1 of the same year, replacing the reimbursement limits passed in 1982 after only a year of operation. Each hospital would come under the plan at the beginning of its usual fiscal year.

What Congress Expected from Prospective Payment

From the beginning prospective payment was recognized as a revolutionary change in medicare. Congress and others expected it to produce major changes for the program and for the medical sector generally.[9]

First and foremost, Congress wanted something that would make federal expenditures under medicare more predictable and controllable than they had been in the past. Since hospital costs accounted for about 70 percent of medicare's total spending, change had to begin with them. Prospective payment—rates set in advance and, after the phase-in period, without reference to the costs incurred by an individual hospital—offered predictability and a greater degree of control.[10]

Second, Congress expected that hospitals would react to the new payment system by becoming more efficient. It was widely believed that hospitals had grown inefficient and wasteful under cost reimbursement and that the same services could be produced more cheaply.

Many people believed that greater efficiency would be enough to keep costs below the rates. With improved efficiency, hospitals would be able to provide more care for the same money. Senator David Durenberger stated, "Efficient hospitals will be able to give beneficiaries more for the money, and that is good for both patients and taxpayers." [11]

Third, many people realized that limits on payment might also give hospitals incentives to cut beneficial services in order to reduce their costs. If the limits were strict, efficiency might not be enough. Congressional concern about maintaining the quality of care led to the creation, in the 1982 legislation, of Peer Review Organizations to monitor quality. Although some of those involved seemed to believe that cuts in quality, while possible, were not inevitable, Senator Lloyd Bentsen warned, "What, in effect, you are going to see is a rationing of health care by its very economics." [12]

What This Book Is About

Thus the chief issue was posed at the outset. If medicare's expenditures are controlled, must anything of importance be given up in return for the savings, and, if so, what? How well the system makes the trade-off between costs and care is a critical test.

This book is about what has happened since the beginning of prospective payment. It reviews what is known and what needs to be learned to arrive at an assessment of prospective payment. Its main purpose is to bring to a larger audience the evaluations, some quite technical, that are being done of the system, in order to contribute to informed debate over a reform that is of foremost importance not only to medicare but to the whole medical system in the United States.

Chapter 2 describes the main characteristics of the new payment plan, sometimes called the PPS (for prospective payment system), in enough detail to allow the reader to understand its consequences better. Chapter 3 looks at how prospective payment has changed the pattern of medical services, reducing inpatient hospital care and increasing the use of other kinds of services. Chapter 4 considers what is known about how those changes have affected the health of beneficiaries—half of the important trade-off between costs and care. Chapter 5 looks at the other half of the trade-off, the effects of prospective payment on the outlays of the medicare program, on payments by beneficiaries, and on the financial condition of hospitals.

Chapter 6 tackles the job of deciding what it all means. Has the growth in medicare's expenditures been slowed enough? On balance, have the effects on the organization of medical resources been good or bad? If valuable things have been given up—new services, access to care—are they a reasonable trade for the lower costs? Is there another way to design the payment system and its administration to reduce any undesirable effects while keeping any good ones? Not everyone will agree with the initial assessment offered here, but the more important purpose of the book—to present the evidence and contribute to the debate—will be served best by offering an assessment of that evidence.

The evidence presented pertains only to the elderly beneficiaries of medicare, some 28 million people, the first and largest group covered by the program. Medicare also covers 3 million disabled people under 65 years of age, including those with end-stage kidney disease. These people represent a special population worthy of a separate investigation to determine how well their needs are met by the new system. That investigation is not attempted in this book.

The reader should also be aware that there is a pervasive problem with trying to decide which phenomena are a consequence of prospective payment and the Peer Review Organizations, and which simply happened at the same time.* The difficulty arises because prospective payment was implemented nationwide, omitting only the hospitals in four states with their own rate-setting programs—New Jersey, Maryland, New York, and Massachusetts. Hospitals in these northeastern states are not typical of those across the nation and, in any event, were not being paid on the basis of costs. Thus there is no comparison group of cost-reimbursed hospitals that can be matched with hospitals under prospective payment.

Some help is provided by the staggered schedule of implementation—hospitals were brought under the system at the start of their usual fiscal year, so that some started on October 1, 1983, while others waited as late as September 1984. For this brief period hospitals already under prospective payment can be compared with those not yet under it. The comparison is imperfect, since cost reimbursement was subject to limits in the year before prospective payment started, but it does help identify effects that were large and immediate.

---

* It is virtually impossible to distinguish the effects of prospective rates from the effects of the Peer Review Organizations, which are operated in conjunction with them. Thus the effects reported in this book should be attributed to the prospective payment system as a whole.

Effects that are taking place more slowly can be hard to distinguish from the general sweep of history. For these, comparisons of trends before and after the introduction of the new system, and comparisons of trends for medicare beneficiaries with those for people under 65 years of age, coupled with reasonable expectations about how prospective payment ought to affect hospitals, can help to identify the system's consequences. These approaches are not, however, free of problems. The insurers and public programs that cover people under 65 have pursued new cost-containment initiatives of their own in the 1980s. Further, it appears that prospective payment's effects may extend beyond the medicare population to other groups. The identification of many of the system's effects thus remains uncertain and must be recognized as such.

CHAPTER TWO

How Prospective Rates Work

THE CRUCIAL features of medicare's prospective payment system are that payment *is* prospective—rates are set before services are delivered—and that a single lump-sum rate pays for the entire hospital stay. The system recognizes, however, that the costs of caring for patients differ from one hospital to the next for a variety of legitimate reasons. To accommodate these differences, rate setting takes into account, along with the patient's diagnosis, certain characteristics of the hospital that are associated with differences in cost, mainly whether it is in an urban or rural area, hospital wage rates in the area, whether it is a teaching hospital, and the proportion of low-income people it serves.

If the hospital can take care of the patient for less than the fixed rate, it keeps the profit. If not, it absorbs the loss. The hospital thus has every reason to produce services as cheaply as possible, omit services where possible, shorten stays, and arrange for some of the patient's care to be given outside the hospital, by a home health agency for example. Even with these efforts, care for some patients will inevitably cost more than the payment rate, but the rates are set with the expectation that a reasonably efficient hospital will profit more often than it will lose.

A new administrative apparatus was created to monitor the operation of the system. Each hospital signs up with a Peer Review Organization, which checks the accuracy of its reports, the appropriateness of decisions to admit and discharge patients, and the quality of care delivered. Monitoring of admissions was started to counter the obvious incentive for hospitals to boost revenues by admitting more patients, monitoring of discharges and quality to guard against the possibility that hospitals would become overzealous in cost cutting and curtail services of real importance to the patient's well-being.

This chapter describes the mechanics of the prospective payment system. Its purpose is not to cover every detail, but to give a realistic sense of the complexity of the system, complexity that necessarily arises when a simple idea meets the variety of the real world. The chapter ends with a discussion of several current issues concerning the design of the payment system.

What's Covered, What's Not

Most but not all hospitals in the United States are included in the prospective payment system.[1] Federal hospitals, such as those run by the Department of Defense and the Veterans' Administration, are excluded. The patient classification system used to calculate rates was considered inappropriate for psychiatric, rehabilitation, children's, and long-term care hospitals, and for psychiatric and rehabilitation units in acute-care hospitals. Such hospitals and units are exempt until systems can be devised for them; in the meantime they continue to be paid their costs, subject to a limit on the rate of increase permitted each year. Alcohol and drug abuse hospitals and units were also excluded at first, but were brought under prospective payment in fiscal 1988.[2] Several states already had systems in place for setting rates that applied to all payers, not just medicare, and four of these were allowed to continue under special waivers. Maryland hospitals are still exempt, but hospitals in Massachusetts and New Jersey, and most of those in New York, have now been included in the medicare system.[3]

Once prospective payment officially began on October 1, 1983, each eligible hospital was brought under it at the beginning of the hospital's next fiscal year. Thus a hospital with a fiscal year beginning on July 1 did not begin to be paid prospectively until July 1, 1984, nine months after the starting date. By the end of September 1984, nearly all hospitals required to participate in PPS were doing so, some 5,400.[4]

The payment rates are designed to cover hospitals' inpatient operating costs. These include costs for room and board, nursing care, "ancillary" services such as laboratory tests, and intensive care.[5] The major omitted items are the costs of capital and the direct costs of medical education. Capital costs—interest, depreciation, and the like—were considered too difficult to include in the rates right away. At the direction of Congress, the secretary of health and human services developed a plan to phase capital payments into the prospective rates over a period of 11 years.[6] Scheduled to go into effect on October 1, 1987, the plan was delayed by Congress, with the result that capital expenses are still paid on the basis of costs, subject to congressionally imposed limits on the percentage of costs that is reimbursed. In fiscal 1987, 96.5 percent of capital costs were reimbursed, 88 percent during most of fiscal 1988, and 85 percent in fiscal 1989.[7] Direct medical education costs, basically the salaries of interns, residents, and other trainees, are also paid at cost; in 1985 Congress directed that prospective rates be developed to pay for the costs of interns and residents, but the system for doing so has not yet been completed.

The Patient Classification System: Diagnosis-Related Groups

The foundation for medicare's prospective rates is a patient classification system called Diagnosis-Related Groups (DRGs), which sorts patients into groups according to medical condition.[8] DRGs were developed at Yale University in the late 1960s. In 1979 the Department of Health and Human Services awarded Yale a grant to develop an improved set of DRGs that would build on experience with the original set. Groups were included in the new set only if they made medical sense to an advisory panel of physicians and differed significantly in cost from other groups when tested against data on hospital admissions. The use of a particular surgical procedure, such as a coronary artery bypass graft, is a defining characteristic of many of the groups. The prospective rate is the same for every patient in a given group, regardless of how long the patient stays in the hospital or what else is done during the stay.

The DRGs used by medicare classify patients using the patient's principal diagnosis, the principal surgical procedure if surgery was performed, whether substantial complicating conditions (called "complications and comorbidities") are present, and the type of discharge.[9] Advanced age (70 or older) was also used in some of the DRGs but was recently dropped after research studies showed complicating conditions, not age, to be the important factor.[10] The report form used for payment allows as many as five conditions and three procedures to be considered in selecting the most appropriate DRG for a given patient. Diagnoses and procedures are identified by codes defined in the International Classification of Diseases (Ninth Revision, Clinical Modification), which is due for its next revision in 1995.[11] The use of these codes marks the first time that all acute-care hospitals in the United States have employed the same codes to report cases for payment.

TABLE 2-1. Selected Diagnosis-Related Groups

DRG number	Title	Fiscal 1988 weight
10	Nervous system neoplasms with complications or comorbidities	1.2123
11	Nervous system neoplasms without complications or comorbidities	0.7729
106	Coronary bypass with cardiac catheterization	5.5415
107	Coronary bypass without cardiac catheterization	4.2858
127	Heart failure and shock	1.0222
176	Complicated peptic ulcer	0.9964
236	Fractures of hip and pelvis	0.9036
317	Admit for renal [kidney] dialysis	0.3542
433	Alcohol or drug abuse or dependence, left hospital against medical advice	0.4232
469[a]	Principal diagnosis invalid as discharge diagnosis	0.0000
470[a]	Ungroupable	0.0000
474[b]	Tracheostomy	11.8772
475[b]	Mechanical ventilation through endotracheal intubation	3.1757

SOURCE: Prospective Payment Assessment Commission, *1988 Adjustments to the Medicare Prospective Payment System: Report to the Congress* (Washington, November 1987), app. C.
   a. DRGs 469 and 470 are used to flag the need for additional information about a case, not for payment. ProPAC, *Technical Appendixes to the Report and Recommendations to the Secretary, U.S. Department of Health and Human Services* (Washington, April 1, 1985), pp. 18–19.
   b. DRGs 474 and 475 were new additions for fiscal 1988.

The sample of DRGs in table 2-1 illustrates how groups are defined. Each DRG is assigned a weight that reflects its costs in relation to a standard case. For example, DRG 10, shown in the table, was paid 1.2123 as much as the average medicare case in fiscal 1988. Although the DRGs themselves were developed from data for 1979 for all hospital admissions, the DRG weights used by medicare are based on data for medicare patients specifically. The ones used when prospective payment was introduced were based on a 20 percent sample of medicare records for 1981.[12]

As conditions, treatments, and patterns of care change, the DRGs must change with them. Over a short period, change can be accommodated by reassigning certain kinds of cases to another, more appropriate, DRG; by creating a new DRG; or by changing the weight for a DRG, a process called *reweighting*.[13] It was recognized at the outset that the entire system of weights would need to be calculated anew from time to time; to distinguish it from reweighting, this complete overhaul is referred to as *recalibration*. The recalibration of all the weights ensures that they reflect changes in the use of resources across DRGs brought about by new technologies and new standards of medical practice. The weights were recalibrated for fiscal 1986, as required by law, again for fiscal 1988, and annually thereafter.[14]

When payment depends on the group into which a patient is classified, hospitals have an incentive to report conditions and procedures in a way that gets the patient assigned to the DRG with the highest payment. In recognition of this fact, the DRG system automatically assigns a patient with several surgical procedures to the group for the most expensive procedure related to the principal diagnosis. Under prospective payment, hospitals have changed their record-keeping practices, coding the patient's stay more carefully and completely, and with an eye to the classification that will result, leading to what is called "DRG creep." The average DRG weight rose following the introduction of prospective payment, and careful study revealed that it increased at each hospital just as that hospital entered the prospective payment system.[15] The average has continued to rise each year, with a leveling-off in 1987, thought at first to be part of a longer-term trend, followed by another substantial increase in 1988.*[16]

How Rates Are Calculated

This description of how prospective rates are calculated presents only the main elements of the system. The fully national system, which applied to most hospitals for the first time in fiscal 1988, is described first, followed by a brief mention of transitional devices used to ease the process of adjustment in the early years.[17]

The rate calculation starts with a standardized payment amount per case, which can be thought of as the average cost of a medicare case in an average, nonteaching, hospital.[18] Originally, the fully national payment system was to make use of two such averages: one for all urban hospitals in the United States, and one for all rural hospitals. With the passage of three separate rates of increase for 1988, however, the two became three: one for hospitals in large urban areas, one for hospitals in other urban areas, and one for rural hospitals. These averages include only costs intended to be covered by the payment rates, excluding capital and other costs that are paid separately. The standardized

---

* Some of the changes in classification have been the result of new coding rules promulgated by the Health Care Financing Administration. See Viola B. Latta and Charles Helbing, "Medicare: Short-Stay Hospital Services, by Leading Diagnosis-Related Groups, 1983 and 1985," *Health Care Financing Review*, vol. 10 (Winter 1988), esp. pp. 79–81.

payment amounts now in use are based on medicare data for 1981, the most recent data available at the time prospective payment began. The rise in hospital costs per admission was then used to update these figures to the first year of prospective payment. Since then they have been raised each year by "annual updates" approved by Congress (discussed in more detail later).

To arrive at the payment rate for a given patient in a given hospital, this standardized amount is adjusted in several ways.[19] That part of the average that reflects labor costs, about 75 percent,[20] is adjusted up or down to reflect hospital wages in the area. The new average is then multiplied by the weight associated with the patient's DRG. The hospital can receive extra payment for part of the costs of cases with unusually high costs or long stays, so-called outliers, and these payments are added at this point; the law stipulates that between 5 and 6 percent of total DRG funds should be set aside for outlier cases.[21]

These adjusted rates are then summed for all the medicare cases in the hospital, and two further adjustments are calculated, each one as a percentage of this total. The adjustment for teaching, called the indirect medical education adjustment, is based on statistical analyses showing that after other measurable factors are accounted for, including the salaries of interns and residents, teaching hospitals have higher costs than other hospitals. These higher costs are presumed to be due to more severely ill patients and to a more expensive level of care that is a necessary part of educating health professionals. The estimated difference, 5.8 percent for every 10 interns and residents per 100 beds, was doubled by Congress for purposes of calculating payment rates when prospective payment began, to 11.6 percent. It has been lowered several times since then (to 7.65 percent for 1989 through 1995) and made part of a more complicated formula.[22]

The adjustment for serving a large proportion of low-income patients was introduced during the third year of prospective payment.[23] It is a particularly complicated one, with different groups of hospitals needing different percentages of low-income patients to qualify for an increase, and receiving different increases when they do qualify. Eligibility depends on the sum of two percentages: the percentage of medicare patient days accounted for by people who receive Supplemental Security Income payments, which are federal payments to low-income elderly and disabled people; and the percentage of all patient days (including medicare) accounted for by people eligible for medicaid. The current set of increases is considerably more generous to large urban

TABLE 2-2. Prospective Payment Rates for a Patient with a Fractured Femur, for Illustrative Hospitals in Selected Cities and Rural Areas, Fiscal Year 1988

Rate in dollars

	Indirect medical education measure:[a]				
	0	.10	.10	0	.30
		Share of low-income patients:[b]			
Hospital location[c]	Less than 15%	Less than 15%	20%	30%	35%
New York City	4,622	4,992	5,223	5,084	6,216
Chicago	4,099	4,427	4,632	4,509	5,514
Los Angeles	4,447	4,803	5,025	4,892	5,981
Baltimore	3,812	4,117	4,308	4,194	5,128
Bangor, Maine	3,442	3,717	3,890	3,786	. . .
Kokomo, Indiana	3,565	3,850	4,029	3,922	. . .
Ocala, Florida	3,242	3,501	3,663	3,566	. . .
Midland, Texas	3,904	4,216	4,411	4,294	. . .
Rural Alabama	2,504	2,704	2,704	2,504	. . .
Rural California	3,380	3,651	3,651	3,380	. . .

SOURCE: Author's calculations based on a formula and data provided by the Congressional Budget Office. All items required for the formula—standardized payment amounts, area wage indexes, the DRG weight for a fractured femur (DRG 235)—and the rules for calculating indirect teaching and disproportionate-share adjustments, are for fiscal 1988.

a. The indirect medical education adjustment is based on the number of interns and residents the hospital has per bed. "Minor" teaching hospitals have at least one intern or resident but less than 0.25 per bed. "Major" teaching hospitals have 0.25 or more interns and residents per bed.

b. The adjustment for a disproportionate share of low-income patients is based on the sum of: (1) the patient days accounted for by medicare patients who receive Supplemental Security Income (a program for low-income elderly and disabled people) as a percentage of all medicare patient days in the hospital; and (2) patient days accounted for by medicaid patients, as a percentage of all patient days in the hospital. The value this sum must be before the hospital qualifies for the disproportionate-share adjustment, and the amount of the adjustment, differ by the size and location of the hospital.

c. For all hospitals in the New England and East North Central states, urban hospitals in the West North Central states, and rural hospitals in the Middle and South Atlantic states, transition to fully national rates has been delayed until fiscal 1990. Until then, 15 percent of their rates will be based on the regional averages, 85 percent on the national. See "Medicare Hospital Payments Rise Apr. 1, 46 Cities Get Bigger Boost," McGraw-Hill's Medicine and Health, vol. 42 (April 11, 1988).

hospitals, and very large rural ones, than to small hospitals in either location.[24]

Because of these adjustments, hospitals in different circumstances receive different payment rates for the same patient. The differences can be quite large, as shown by the examples in table 2-2. The wage index determines the level for all hospitals in a given area, and adjustments for teaching programs and a disproportionate share of low-income patients cause further variations in the rates for hospitals in the same area. For treating a patient with a fractured femur, a New York City hospital that had no teaching program and did not qualify for the disproportionate-share adjustment received $4,622 in fiscal 1988, while a hospital in Kokomo, Indiana, received $3,565, and one in rural California received $3,380. If a New York City hospital had one-tenth of an intern or resident per bed, and met all the requirements for the disproportionate-share adjustment with a low-income percentage of 20, its rate rose to $5,223, compared with $4,029 in Kokomo and $3,651 in rural California.

The payment rates are increased from year to year. The increases for the first two years of prospective payment were largely determined by the legislative requirement that total payments be the same as they would have been under the cost limits in effect in 1982. After that the annual updates, as they are called, were to be set by the secretary of health and human services. Congress, however, preempted this role from the start and reclaimed it officially in the Omnibus Budget Reconciliation Act of 1986.[25] The law directs that an annual update be chosen after considering the rate of inflation in prices for hospital goods and services, hospital productivity, advances in technology, the quality of care, and the long-term cost-effectiveness of hospital services.[26] In short, Congress and the secretary are to consider how much of an increase is needed to support good care at a reasonable cost.

The update factors chosen have been much affected by the fact that, on average, hospitals at first made substantial profits under prospective payment (more on this in chapter 5). The profits allayed fears that the quality of care would suffer and raised concerns that rates had been set too high initially. The first column of table 2-3 shows the annual update percentages. The schedule of increases for the latter part of fiscal 1988 (see table note f) reflects a concern that the urban–rural difference is not fair to rural hospitals, so that rural hospitals need larger increases in partial compensation.

The standardized amounts, like the DRG weights, need to be recalculated from time to time as more recent cost data become available, a process called *rebasing*. As of fiscal 1989, no rebasing had been done, and the standardized amounts in use were still based on 1981 data, updated to the price level of 1984 and by the update amounts after that. Some preliminary analyses had, however, been carried out with data from the first year of prospective payment (hospital fiscal years starting after October 1, 1983); the standardized amounts for fiscal 1987 calculated from these more recent data were 12.3 percent lower than those derived from the 1981 data,[27] confirming the suspicion that the rates based on 1981 were too high and setting the stage for continued low annual updates.

In addition to the prospective rate they receive for each medicare

TABLE 2-3. Annual Updates and Percentages for Transition to
Federal Payment Rates, 1984–88

Fiscal year[a]	Annual update	Transition percentages			
		Hospital-specific	Federal[b]	[National	Regional]
1984					
October 1, 1983– September 30, 1984	. . .	75	25	[0	100]
1985					
October 1, 1984– September 30, 1985	3.4	50	50	[25	75]
1986[c]					
October 1, 1985– April 31, 1986	Frozen at 1985	50	50	[25	75]
May 1, 1986– September 30, 1986	0.5	45	55	[25	75]
1987					
October 1, 1986– September 30, 1987	1.15	25	75	[50	50]
1988[d]					
October 1, 1987– November 20, 1987	Frozen at 1987	25	75	[100	0]
November 21, 1987– March 31, 1988	0.4	0	100	[100	0]
April 1, 1988– September 30, 1988[e]	[f]	0	100	[100	0]
or					
	[f]	0	100	[85	15]
1989					
October 1, 1989– September 30, 1990[e]	[f]	0	100	[100	0]
or					
	[f]	0	100	[85	15]

SOURCES: For 1984–87, *Background Material and Data on Programs within the Jurisdiction of the Committee on Ways and Means*, Committee Print WMCP 100-4, House Committee on Ways and Means, 100 Cong. 1 sess. (Government Printing Office, March 1987). For 1988, Cathy Tokarski, "PPS to Get More Complicated April 1," *Modern Healthcare*, vol. 18 (February 19, 1988), p. 24. For update factors, 1984–87, Prospective Payment Assessment Commission, *Report and Recommendations to the Secretary, U.S. Department of Health and Human Services* (Washington, April 1987), pp. 27–28; ProPAC, *1988 Adjustments to the Medicare Prospective Payment System: Report to the Congress* (Washington, November 1987), and *1989 Adjustments to the Medicare Prospective Payment System: Report to the Congress* (Washington, November 1988); 42 C.F.R. sec. 412.71 (1987); and P.L. 99-272, sec. 9102.

a. The hospital-specific and federal percentages change at the beginning of the hospital's fiscal year; the hospital-specific amount is updated at the same time. The first day of the federal fiscal year is the first day on which the new rates could be applied. However, they are not actually applied to hospitals until the beginning of the hospital's fiscal year. (House Ways and Means Committee, *Background Material*, p. 223.)

b. The federal portion of the overall rate is a mixture of varying proportions of national and regional rates, the final target being a federal portion based solely on national rates. The national and regional percentages, which make up the federal portion of the overall rate, change at the beginning of each federal fiscal year. The federal payment amounts are generally updated at the same time. (House Ways and Means Committee, *Background Material*, p. 223; and 42 C.F.R. sec. 412.71.)

patient, hospitals are, as noted, paid separately for capital expenses, direct medical education costs, medicare bad debts, and a few other items.

To give hospitals time to adjust, prospective payment was phased in over several years. During the transition period, payment rates were based on a blend of the hospital's 1982 costs (updated), the national rates just described, and a set of regional rates calculated in the same manner as the national rates for the nine census regions of the country. The original plan was that the hospital's own costs would make up 75 percent of its payment rate in the first transition year, 50 percent in the second, and 25 percent in the third, with the national system in effect in the fourth year. As table 2-3 shows (columns 2–5), actual progress was somewhat slower and more halting, and the transition period was not completely finished for all hospitals even in fiscal 1988.

To accommodate a variety of special circumstances, certain hospitals are paid somewhat differently from most of those under prospective payment. Hospitals that are (or can choose to be) paid differently include those that are the only ones providing care in their area ("sole community provider"); those that, although located in rural areas,

---

TABLE 2-3 *(continued)*

c. For the first seven months of a hospital's cost-reporting period beginning on or after the start of federal fiscal year 1986, the overall payment rate was 50 percent hospital-specific and 50 percent federal. For the last five months of a hospital's cost-reporting period beginning on or after the start of federal fiscal year 1986, the overall payment rate was 45 percent hospital-specific and 55 percent federal rate. (House Ways and Means Committee, *Background Material,* p. 223.)

Full implementation of prospective payment (the transition to 100 percent federal rates) was originally scheduled to occur in fiscal 1986. The Consolidated Omnibus Budget Reconciliation Act of 1985, however, delayed full implementation for one year for all PPS hospitals except those in the state of Oregon. While most PPS hospitals were paid 45 percent of the hospital-specific rate and 55 percent of the federal rate during the last five months of their cost-reporting periods beginning after the start of fiscal 1986, hospitals in Oregon received 25 percent of the hospital-specific rate and 75 percent of the federal rate. This 25-75 split was what had originally been scheduled for all PPS hospitals for fiscal 1986. The national–regional composition of the federal rate was the same for hospitals in Oregon as for all other hospitals under PPS. (P.L. 99-272, sec. 9102.)

d. By act of Congress, PPS payment rates were frozen at fiscal 1987 levels until November 21, 1987, when they were increased by 0.4 percent. (ProPAC, *1988 Adjustments,* p. 6.)

e. From April 1, 1988, through September 30, 1990, hospitals can be paid either 100 percent of the national rate or a combination of 85 percent of the national rate and 15 percent of the regional rate, whichever is higher. For fiscal 1988, the blended 85-15 rate applies to all hospitals in the New England and East North Central states, to urban hospitals in the West North Central states, and to rural hospitals in the Middle and South Atlantic states. (53 Fed. Reg. 11,136 [1988].)

f. The update percentages for the periods April 1–September 30, 1988, and October 1, 1988–September 30, 1989, are as follows:

	April–Sept. 1988	Oct. 88– Sept. 89
Hospitals in metropolitan areas with population over 1 million	1.5	3.4
Other urban hospitals	1.0	2.9
Rural hospitals	3.0	3.9
Hospitals not paid under PPS	2.7	5.4

(Tokarski, "PPS to Get More Complicated," p. 24; and ProPAC, *1989 Adjustments,* p. B-4.)

serve as referral centers for the region or nation; cancer treatment and research centers; and Christian Science sanitoria.[28]

The Rest of the System

Part of the purpose of paying hospitals a fixed rate for a hospital stay is to encourage the use of less-expensive alternatives to hospital care. In the early 1980s, just before the prospective payment system was created, Congress made important changes in the coverage of some of these alternatives.

Surgery performed in freestanding ambulatory surgical centers was covered under medicare for the first time beginning in 1982.[29] Physicians in these centers perform surgical procedures for which the patient does not need to be hospitalized. Unlike hospital-affiliated centers or outpatient departments, where the same kinds of procedures are often performed, freestanding centers, as the name suggests, are not associated with a larger institution, and, until 1982, medicare did not cover them.

In all three types of centers, the physician who performs the surgery and the center usually bill the patient separately; the center's bill covers the cost of the operating room, nursing care, and the like. Because no hospital stay is involved, medicare beneficiaries would ordinarily be required to satisfy the $75 Part B deductible and pay 20 percent of amounts above $75 for procedures performed in these centers. But, to encourage the use of outpatient surgery, Congress waived the deductible and coinsurance on the physician's bill, and on the center's bill for those centers paid prospective rates—freestanding ambulatory surgery centers and some hospital-affiliated centers; the deductible and coinsurance continued to apply to bills from centers paid on the basis of costs.[30] Outpatient surgery rapidly became established, not only because of this favorable financial treatment but also because of technological developments that permitted procedures to be done more easily and safely out of the hospital, and medicare ended the special treatment of centers' bills in 1987 and of physicians' bills in 1988.

Coverage of home health care, which can be used instead of longer hospital stays for some patients, was also made more generous. If the patient's condition meets the requirements for coverage—for example, the patient must be suffering from an acute condition—care is paid for in full, with no deductibles or copayments. Initially, home health services were provided only to patients whose illnesses had first required hospital stays of at least three days, but that requirement was dropped in 1981 (date of implementation), and so was the limit on the number of home health visits for which medicare would pay.[31]

Medicare rarely covers care in nursing homes, and this policy has not changed. The major sources of payment for nursing home care are medicaid and individuals. Medicaid, the federal–state program that helps pay the medical expenses of the poor, has been subject to budget cuts in recent years; changes made in the program in 1981 allowed states to experiment with using home health care as an alternative to nursing homes, but did not change nursing home coverage in any other way. As a result, coverage of nursing home stays has been much the same in the period of prospective payment as before—no special attempts have been made to encourage its use.[32]

Of the organizational changes that accompanied prospective payment, perhaps the most important was the creation of a network of Peer Review Organizations (PROs) to monitor hospital performance.[33] Under contracts with the Health Care Financing Administration, the agency of the Department of Health and Human Services that administers medicare, PROs review admissions to verify the reported diagnosis and procedure codes to determine whether admissions and procedures were necessary, and to check on cases submitted for outlier payments. They are also responsible for reviewing the quality of care, a responsibility that was broadened in the second round of contracts. (Their role in ensuring quality is considered in chapter 4.)

PROs review a random sample of individual admissions to check on the need for the admission, the quality of the care provided, and the accuracy of the hospital's coding. At first they also reviewed quarterly reports from each hospital showing data on all admissions, but this review was discontinued. They are required to review all readmissions that occur within a short time of the original hospital discharge— readmissions are considered an indicator that the care given during the first stay may have been inadequate. In addition, PROs select specific types of admissions and procedures to receive special attention, the choice depending on the suspected weaknesses of hospitals in the area; for example, in the first year of prospective payment, all PROs were required to review pacemaker implantations because of reports that they were often done unnecessarily.[34]

The responsibilities of PROs are gradually being extended beyond the hospital. In August 1987 they began to review care provided to medicare beneficiaries in health maintenance organizations. Home health care, outpatient surgery, nursing home care, and, ultimately, physicians' offices will be added in turn. A limited review of posthospital care has already begun in the form of reviews of the care received by patients who were discharged from a hospital and then readmitted within a month.

Congress also created a special agency at the time prospective payment was enacted, the Prospective Payment Assessment Commission, to study the system and make recommendations for its improvement. The commission advises Congress and the secretary of health and human services on the appropriate annual update and the need for changes in the DRG classification system as well as on other matters. Consisting of 17 members and staff, the commission is a congressional agency. It prepares three annual reports, one presenting its recommendations and supporting studies, one discussing the impact of prospective payment on the medical care system, and one commenting on the changes made in prospective payment each year by the secretary.[35]

Issues

The costs of caring for patients differ from one hospital to the next for a variety of reasons. The prospective payment system recognizes only some of those reasons as legitimate. It tries to allow for the legitimate reasons in the way rates are set and to avoid paying for other differences in costs. The important issues about the mechanics of prospective payment—how the rates are and should be set—have to do with determining the differences in costs among hospitals, deciding which are legitimate for payment, and devising ways to incorporate the legitimate ones into the payment system.

Five variables are used to set the payment rate for a given patient in a given hospital: the location of the hospital (urban or rural); hospital wages in the area; the patient's diagnosis-related group; the size of the hospital's teaching program; and the share of low-income patients served by the hospital. Additional payments are made if the patient is an outlier, that is, has an exceptionally long stay or exceptionally high costs. One study has estimated that the fully national rate system, based on the five variables plus outlier payments, would have accounted for over 70 percent of the variation in costs among hospitals in 1984.[36]

The recurring policy question is, What accounts for the remaining variation? Is it inefficiency, something medicare explicitly does not want to pay for? Or is it at least in part due to some other factor that medicare would agree to recognize if it were identified? A related but somewhat more technical question is whether the factors used measure legitimate differences accurately.

Except for wages, the variables used to determine payment rates are implicit, and imperfect, adjustments for the severity of illness of the patients in a particular hospital and for the kind of care they receive. Outlier payments provide another way to recognize severity in un-usual cases that are not well represented by the five payment variables. It has been argued repeatedly, however, that the system still does not fully adjust for differences in the severity of patients' illnesses. A more severely ill patient—defined[37] as one who, at the time of admission to the hospital, has a greater chance of a poor outcome—can reasonably be expected to be more costly to treat. Thus if it could be shown that PPS does not accurately recognize differences in severity of illness, and if a way to measure this severity could be found, the architects of pro-spective payment would be willing to adjust the system to reflect the new information.

Several classification systems have been proposed as replacements for, or refinements of, the DRG system.[38] All of them, including DRGs, face a common problem. Both in principle and in practice, it is difficult to devise a way of measuring severity that reflects only the patient's condition and not what is done for the patient. Measuring what is done for the patient comes back to measuring costs, and the whole purpose of prospective payment is to get away from reimbursing costs. Although a few of the systems are more purely based on the patient's condition than are DRGs, a recent report prepared for Congress con-cludes that none perform better than DRGs in explaining differences in costs among hospitals. Thus none of them is yet good enough to replace DRGs.

They offer more promise as a way to refine DRGs by subdividing them into smaller groups that are more truly alike in severity. The au-thors of the report conclude that "a series of modest improvements appear possible, and may, in combination, produce even larger im-provements."[39] The method of Disease Staging looks most promising to them. Disease Staging sorts patients into diagnostic groups and then further divides them according to the stage of the disease (1 through 4), with higher-numbered stages representing more serious disease.

The technique uses data that are already collected for prospective payment and, when combined with DRGs, improves their ability to sort patients into groups with similar costs. It remains to be seen whether this greater precision would actually make a difference to the total payments received by a hospital or whether it would simply shift the money around among patients without affecting the hospital's total.

While most people would be willing to incorporate finer adjustments for the severity of illness if such adjustments could be made, it is less obvious to what extent prospective payment should pay for differences in the care delivered to essentially similar patients. Clearly the system should not pay for more costly care if it fails to produce a better outcome for the patient. The difficult questions arise when care is more expensive but also more effective, or when, as is often the case, the effectiveness of more expensive care is not known. Another difficult question is whether medicare should pay for differences in care that arise because the patient or doctor prefers the more expensive alternative. Nothing about the prospective payment system, of course, prevents the hospital from providing whatever care the physician and patient want, but if more expensive technologies are not reflected in higher rates, the hospital will find it difficult to do so very often and still cover its costs.

The Health Care Financing Administration, the arm of the Department of Health and Human Services that administers medicare, is beginning to consider the possibility that the prospective rates should pay for more expensive care only if it is also more effective *and* if the greater effect is considered worth the expense. It will hold a series of consensus conferences to review the costs and effects of expensive technologies and recommend decisions about each one.[40]

Other policy issues about the design of prospective payment rates are also variations on the same general theme: do the rates recognize the cost differences they should and do so accurately? As another example, a number of changes have been made, or proposed, in the indexes used to adjust for wage differences among areas, with the aim of measuring these differences more accurately. In its first four annual reports the Prospective Payment Assessment Commission proposed that the labor market areas for which indexes are calculated should be defined more narrowly.[41] In particular, the commission suggests that each urban area, currently treated as a single labor market, should be subdivided into central city and suburban labor markets to recognize the higher labor costs of central city hospitals. Similarly, they propose that rural areas should be subdivided into urbanized rural and other rural sections.

Payment for rural hospitals is an issue of growing importance in the annual debates over the direction of prospective payment.[42] Because rural hospitals have lower costs than urban ones, separate standardized amounts are used for the two groups of hospitals. The reasons for the cost gap are not fully known or understood but include differences in the sophistication of services offered by these hospitals and in the severity of illness of their patients, the latter not fully captured by DRGs. Thus the urban–rural difference is a proxy for severity, an accepted reason for different costs, and for intensity of care.[43]

Initially the standardized amount for urban hospitals was about 25 percent higher than the amount for rural hospitals.[44] Spokesmen for rural hospitals complained that the differential was too great and that, in any event, it was not justified.[45] It has been reduced by recent legislation to about 17 percent in 1988, and 12 or 13 percent in 1989. Calculations by the Prospective Payment Assessment Commission suggest that this may be about right—they show that average cost per case was 14 percent higher in urban hospitals than in rural ones during the first year of prospective payment.[46] Even so, the commission argues that the issue of whether there should be an urban–rural differential at all should be reassessed.

Not all of the changes, of course, are made on the basis of what is the best national policy. Some are simply the result of political favors to hospitals with powerful backers. In the negotiations over rate increases for fiscal 1988, for example, Congress agreed to give Providence, Rhode Island, the rate increase scheduled for urban areas with more than 1 million inhabitants, although Providence falls short of that mark, and to allow two Alabama counties to be considered urban, although they do not meet the criteria for urban areas, so that they can qualify for the higher urban rates.

A complete list would include these issues and many more—the appropriate indexes for measuring inflation in the prices of goods and services bought by hospitals, the measurement and weighting of the factors considered in deriving annual updates, the best way to adjust rates for new technologies, and so on. How these issues are resolved influences hospitals' decisions about what services to invest in, what people to employ, and how to care for patients. The discussion of the few examples given here has been too brief to give the reader a full understanding of the arguments, or of all the elements that must be balanced in arriving at a conclusion. Instead, their purpose is, as with the description of the rate system itself, to give a realistic sense of the kinds of issues that come up and the framework within which changes are made.

CHAPTER THREE

Changes in the Pattern of Medical Services

CONGRESS approved prospective payment in part because it believed that hospitals, and the medical sector generally, were inefficient. It was widely believed, well beyond the halls of Congress, that hospitals could produce the same services, or at least the same outcomes, more cheaply, but that as long as they were paid their costs they would feel no pressure to do so. Prospectively set rates would force them to become more efficient in order to stay in business. In the process, hospitals would not only modify their own operations but would take the lead in changing the mix of services provided by the entire medical care sector, making less use of expensive inpatient care and more use of such substitutes as nursing homes, home health services, and outpatient care. Many people believed that these changes could cut costs substantially without adversely affecting patients' health. Whether this is true is an open question, one that will be considered in the next chapter. This chapter looks at the pattern of medical services before and after the implementation of prospective payment.

Prospective payment has led to fundamental changes in medical care in the few short years since its introduction. As predicted, the use of inpatient care has dropped sharply, and the use of substitutes has increased. Hospital admissions of the elderly have declined for the first time since medicare began, and in spite of expectations that they would rise; this result can be attributed in part to the watchdog efforts of the Department of Health and Human Services. Lengths of stay fell sharply in the first year—from 9.7 days in 1983 to 8.6 days in 1984, much more than expected on the basis of previous trends. With fewer medicare patients being hospitalized, it seems likely that those still in the hospital are more seriously ill, yet the use of intensive care dropped in 1984 before rebounding to its earlier level in 1985.

Many more medicare patients are being referred to home health care when they leave the hospital, but it appears that the expected increase in discharges to nursing homes may not have occurred. Amid claims that their patients are sicker than in the past, both nursing homes and home health agencies are increasingly providing more skilled services; this trend predated prospective payment and the evidence is insufficient to show what part the new payment system has played in shaping it. The use of outpatient surgery is up sharply. Much more of doctors' services are now provided in the outpatient departments of hospitals and in their offices rather than in hospital wards: in 1982, 61 percent of the physicians' bills paid by medicare was for care given to hospital inpatients, but by 1986 that had dropped to less than 50 percent.

Medicare supplies almost 30 percent of hospitals' revenues[1] and when medicare changes, the medical industry changes. In the era of prospective payment, hospitals find themselves, for the first time in decades, reducing the number of beds and cutting inpatient employment; they have rapidly expanded their outpatient services. Despite the cutbacks in inpatient facilities, occupancy rates are at an all-time low.

The rest of the chapter describes these changes in more detail. The sections consider in turn inpatient hospital care; the use of posthospital services, principally nursing homes and home health care; and physicians' services and outpatient surgery.

Inpatient Hospital Services

One of the most widely held expectations about prospective payment was that it would cause admissions to increase. Because admissions for people aged 65 or older had increased every year from the time medicare began (table 3-1), another increase seemed a certainty even if nothing else changed. Prospective payment provided a reason to make the increase larger than usual: with payment per case fixed, hospitals could earn more revenue by admitting more patients. The report to Congress proposing the prospective payment system stated the matter carefully: "Because the case (discharge) is the unit of service, the hospital may have an incentive to increase admissions, in order to contribute to overhead, as long as the DRG payment rate is greater than the marginal cost of producing a case."[2] The marginal cost refers to those costs that are incurred only if a patient enters the hospital; many costs, such as those to maintain beds and nurses to staff them, are the same whether or not an additional patient is admitted, at least in the short run.

TABLE 3-1. Medicare Admissions and Length of Stay
in Short-Stay Hospitals, 1967–88[a]

Year	Total admissions (thousands)	Admissions per 1,000 aged enrollees	Average length of stay
		Medicare data (medicare enrollees aged 65 or older)[b]	
1967	5,313	275	13.8
1968	5,823	297	13.8
1969	6,090	306	13.5
1970	6,139	304	13.0
1971	6,318	307	12.5
1972	6,610	316	12.1
1973	6,861	321	11.7
1974	7,160	328	11.5
1975	7,404	332	11.2
1976	7,801	343	11.1
1977	8,123	349	10.9
1978	8,389	353	10.8
1979	8,662	356	10.7
1980	9,258	369	10.6
1981	9,648	377	10.4
1982	10,084	386	10.1
1983	10,462	392	9.7
1984	10,331	381	8.6
		National Hospital Panel Survey data (all people aged 65 or older)[b]	
1983	11,812	n.a.	9.7
1984	11,508	n.a.	8.9
1985	10,904	n.a.	8.8
1986	10,795	n.a.	8.8
1987	10,841	n.a.	8.9
1988	11,062	n.a.	8.8

SOURCES: Total medicare admissions and admissions per 1,000 enrollees from Bureau of the Census, *Statistical Abstract of the United States, 1972*, p. 293; *1977*, p. 336; *1978*, p. 347; *1981*, p. 335; *1984*, p. 386; *1985*, p. 372; *1987*, p. 357. Length of stay, 1967–81, from Health Care Financing Administration, Office of Research and Demonstrations, *Report to Congress: Impact of the Medicare Hospital Prospective Payment System, 1985 Annual Report*, Pub. 03251 (Baltimore: U.S. Department of Health and Human Services, August 1987), table 3.7a; and Susan DesHarnais and others, "The Early Effects of the Prospective Payment System on Inpatient Utilization and the Quality of Care," *Inquiry*, vol. 24 (Spring 1987), table 2. National Hospital Panel Survey data supplied by the American Hospital Association.

n.a. Not available.

a. Data include the states exempt from prospective payment ("waiver states").

b. Admissions for all people 65 or older, as reported by the National Hospital Panel Survey, are larger than medicare admissions for enrollees 65 or older for several reasons: not all elderly people are covered by medicare; the panel survey may include admissions to hospital units that are excluded from prospective payment and therefore not included in medicare's numbers; admissions of patients enrolled in health maintenance organizations are not always reported to medicare even though they are supposed to be.

Because it was well aware of this possibility, the Health Care Financing Administration prepared to counter it. In the first three-quarters of the year during which hospitals were subject to cost limits under the Tax Equity and Fiscal Responsibility Act of 1982 (TEFRA), even before prospective payment began, the HCFA reviewed summary reports on each hospital's admissions and identified more than a thousand with "unusual" increases. These hospitals were investigated further, and many were required to develop plans to correct the situation.[3] Later, in the first round of contracts with the Peer Review Organizations (PROs), the HCFA put major emphasis on reviewing admissions.[4] The PROs were, and still are, required to review a sample of admissions from each hospital in detail; if a sufficiently high percentage of the admissions reviewed are considered unjustified, all the hospital's medicare admissions are reviewed. At first PROs were also required to continue the review of quarterly summaries from each hospital, but that requirement was dropped during the contract period. In addition, each PRO selects five procedures for preadmission review—pacemaker implants must now be one of the five—and hospitals must agree to deny the patient admission if the PRO decides against it.[5] Considerable stress is placed on keeping surgical cases out of the hospital whenever it is safe to do the surgery on an outpatient basis. Medicare administrators underlined the seriousness of this effort by warning that, if admissions grew too much, increases in the payment rates would be restrained to make up the difference.[6]

The effort was so successful that admissions declined in the first year of prospective payment. While no two sources measure admissions exactly the same way, all agree that admissions of elderly people declined between 1983 and 1984 (table 3-1), the first year of prospective payment (although recall that not all hospitals were under prospective payment until the fall of 1984). Admissions covered by medicare show a decline of just over 1 percent. Data on a more inclusive count of hospital stays, those for all people aged 65 or older whether or not they are covered by medicare, are more current than the medicare statistics. They too show a decline between 1983 and 1984, and they show that admissions continued to decline through 1986 before rising modestly in the next two years to a level still well below that of 1983.

Much of the decline can be traced to the shift to outpatient surgery encouraged by the Peer Review Organizations, and especially to a massive shift in the location of cataract surgery. For example, 37 PROs included lens procedures, principally cataract removal and the insertion of intraocular lenses, which are usually done at the same time, on their lists of procedures requiring preadmission review.[7] A study of 646 hospitals over the period 1980 through 1985 found that admissions for lens procedures fell from 15,000 in 1983 to 11,000 in 1984 and 2,000 in 1985;[8] this category alone accounted for 54 percent of the decline in admissions for these hospitals between 1984 and 1985.

Because of the decline in total admissions, admissions per 1,000 elderly enrollees declined in 1984, also for the first time since the medicare program began. The admission rate had risen steadily from 275 per 1,000 enrollees in 1967 to 392 per 1,000 in 1983, an increase of more than 40 percent. In 1984 it dropped back to 381 per 1,000 and, as is clear from the data for total admissions, continued to drop for the next several years.

The medicare pattern, a steady rise historically followed by declines during the early years of the new payment system, was not mirrored by changes in the younger population—another reason to attribute it to the efforts of the PROs. Admissions for people under age 65 declined steadily for several years before prospective payment. Perhaps influenced by spillover effects from medicare, perhaps by cost-containment efforts being pursued by other third-party payers, admissions for this group fell somewhat faster in 1984 and 1985, although not at rates out of line with previous years.[9]

The average length of stay in the hospital for medicare patients behaved exactly as predicted, dropping sharply in the first year of prospective payment (table 3-1). Again, different sources give different numbers, but all tell the same story. The numbers in table 3-1 include the states exempted from prospective payment, states with historically long lengths of stay, so the averages are higher than for prospective payment states alone.[10] Nonetheless, they show a drop from 9.7 days in 1983 to 8.6 days in 1984 for elderly medicare patients. In contrast to admissions, virtually all of the decline in lengths of stay took place in the first year, with the average stable thereafter.

Historically, length of stay for the elderly had declined steadily, drifting slowly downward from 13.8 days in 1968 to 10.1 days in 1982 (table 3-1). The declines in the two years before prospective payment were unusually steep by historical standards, but the decline between 1983 and 1984, when the average dropped by nearly a day, was unprecedented, ample reason to suspect that prospective payment was the cause. A study of Philadelphia hospitals found that both prospective payment and the TEFRA cost limits that preceded it reduced stays, with the impact of prospective payment greater than that of the cost limits, and that both reductions were statistically significant.[11]

The decline in lengths of stay was remarkably consistent across the nation. Hospitals in the western states have traditionally had shorter stays than those elsewhere, and it made sense to expect that they would reduce their stays less than other hospitals, if at all. Yet stays in the West also dropped sharply under prospective payment, and even after those elsewhere had leveled off, stays for surgical cases in the West continued to decline.[12]

These shorter stays reflect the pressures put on physicians by hospitals. In a 1984 nationwide survey, almost two-thirds of physicians reported that they were encouraged to discharge patients sooner.[13] In addition, three-quarters of the specialists in radiology, anesthesiology, and pathology indicated that, because of prospective payment, they were encouraged to do more testing without admitting the patient to the hospital. This practice also helps to reduce stays for patients who are later hospitalized, since test results are already available.

Exactly where have the cuts in stays occurred? The shift of easier, short-stay cases, such as cataract surgery, to outpatient settings would have produced longer average hospital stays had nothing else been done, simply because the patients still being hospitalized are those whose conditions require longer stays. Thus, to reduce average stays as much as they did, hospitals had to cut the stays of longer-stay patients, and by enough to make up for the loss of some shorter-stay patients to outpatient care. Data from case studies show how this may have occurred. A study of hip fracture patients in one Indiana teaching hospital reported that the average stay for these patients dropped from 16.6 days in the three years before prospective payment to 10.3 days for 1984 and 1985.[14] A community hospital in Indiana experienced an even sharper drop for hip fracture patients, from 21.9 days to 12.6.[15] An exploratory study of mastectomy patients found that the hospital stay could be reduced from 9.7 days to 2.7 days.[16] In all cases, the shorter stays meant that some services previously provided during the stay were provided outside the hospital.

It is impossible, however, to supply a more general answer to the question. In principle, a comparison of stays in each diagnosis-related group before and under prospective payment could show where cuts have occurred. In practice, the more complete information now used to classify patients, and the incentives hospitals have to report that information in a way that yields the highest payment rate for each patient, produced large shifts among DRGs in the first few years of the new payment system.[17] As a result the patients in a given DRG are not comparable from year to year, and it is therefore not valid to compare lengths of stay for the same DRG. Only more time-consuming approaches, such as that used by the authors of the hip fracture study, who reviewed patients' medical records to ensure that they selected the same kinds of patients for each year, can overcome the problem.

For the same reasons, it is difficult to test the expectation that medicare patients admitted to hospitals under prospective payment are more seriously ill than those admitted in the recent past. It is reasonable to believe that they are. More patients are being treated as outpatients, and these are presumably the ones who would have been the simpler, less severely ill cases in the hospital before prospective payment. Those who are admitted in the era of prospective payment should thus be the more seriously ill and in need of more sophisticated services.

Although medicare patients in hospitals probably are sicker now, the use of intensive care and coronary care units, referred to collectively as intensive care, appears to have declined in the first year of prospective payment. These units monitor patients who are critically ill and provide intensive therapy and life support; coronary care units specialize in heart patients, while intensive care units admit the full range of medical and surgical conditions. After its first appearance in the early 1960s, intensive care grew rapidly, accounting for 5 percent of hospital beds in 1975 and 8 percent in 1985.[18] The use of intensive care specifically for medicare patients rose each year during the early 1980s.[19]

During the first year of prospective payment, 1984, the use of intensive care for medicare patients fell. One study found that the number of intensive care admissions reported on medicare bills declined 6 percent in fiscal 1984 and that stays in these units, which had been stable in the preceding three years, also declined.[20]

Two other studies report the percentages of medicare patients who received care in an intensive or coronary care unit during their hospital stay.[21] Both studies are based on essentially the same sample of hospitals in states subject to prospective payment, but they present intensive care data only for those that reported such data for the entire study period. Because of this requirement, fewer hospitals are included in the study that covers the longer period (see table 3-2). A 10 percent sample

TABLE 3-2. Use of Intensive Care by Medicare Patients, 1980–84 and 1980–85

Item	Before prospective payment				Under prospective payment	
	1980	1981	1982	1983	1984	1985
Intensive care units[a]						
Patients	2,845	3,347	3,312	3,522	3,002	...
Percent of total admissions	8.98	9.35	9.42	9.61	8.66*	...
Adjusted percent[b]	...	...	...	...	7.82*	...
Coronary care units[c]						
Patients	2,855	3,271	3,210	3,467	2,915	...
Percent of total admissions	9.01	9.14	9.13	9.46	8.41*	...
Adjusted percent[b]	...	...	...	...	7.59*	...
Intensive care units[d]						
Patients	2,602	2,856	3,066	3,216	3,057	3,289
Percent of total admissions	9.14	9.63	9.76	9.87	9.87	11.23
Adjusted percent[b]	...	...	...	...	8.98*	9.27
Coronary care units[e]						
Patients	2,594	2,812	2,883	3,203	2,986	3,254
Percent of total admissions	9.11	9.48	9.18	9.83	9.64	11.11
Adjusted percent[b]	...	...	...	...	8.77	9.17

SOURCES: Top half of table from DesHarnais and others, "Early Effects of the Prospective Payment System," p. 10. Bottom half of table from Susan DesHarnais, James Chesney, and Steven Fleming, "The Impact of the Prospective Payment System on Hospital Utilization and the Quality of Care: Trends and Regional Variations in the First Two Years," paper presented at the October 1987 meeting of the American Public Health Association, table 2.
*Significantly different from trend. Probability is less than .05 that such a large difference could occur by chance.
a. Based on 424 hospitals that reported data for all five years.
b. Patients admitted to intensive care divided by the total number of admissions that would have occurred in the absence of prospective payment. Projected admissions were taken from cited sources.
c. Based on 373 hospitals that reported data for all five years.
d. Based on 368 hospitals that reported data for all six years.
e. Based on 324 hospitals that reported data for all six years.

of discharges was drawn from each hospital for the third quarter of each year; thus the 1983 discharges occurred before prospective payment went into effect, while hospitals were still under the TEFRA cost limits, and the 1984 discharges occurred in the last three months of the first year of prospective payment, by which time most hospitals were included. The data come from the files of the Commission on Professional and Hospital Activities, an organization whose members pay for the privilege of receiving profiles based on their own data and that of other member hospitals. With its large membership, and data that go back many years, the CPHA provides a reliable and reasonably representative picture of what is happening in the nation's hospitals.

The percentages must be interpreted carefully. By definition, they are calculated as the number of patients receiving intensive care, divided by the total number of patients admitted to the hospital. Since the total number of patients admitted has declined under prospective payment, the percentage receiving intensive care would go up *even if no more patients were admitted to these units than before*; if the patients still admitted to hospitals in the prospective payment era are those who are most seriously ill, it would make sense that the number of intensive care admissions would remain the same even as total admissions dropped.* To adjust for this problem, table 3-2 reports both the published percentages from one of the articles and adjusted percentages calculated using estimates of the admissions that would have occurred without prospective payment.

It appears from these two studies that the use of intensive care fell during the first year of prospective payment, as the medicare bills indicate, and then returned to its earlier level in 1985. The number of patients admitted to intensive and coronary care units rose nearly every year before the introduction of prospective payment, dropped sharply in 1983–84, then rose again in 1984–85, to levels slightly above those of 1983. The pattern suggests that hospitals may have reacted quickly to the new payment system, cutting back on intensive care admissions to control costs, and then decided both that they could afford the admissions and that they were worthwhile for patients.

Further evidence for this temporary decline is provided by a statistical analysis of patients in eight diagnosis-related groups.[22] The authors found that the probability of being admitted to intensive care declined from 1983 to 1984 for patients in most of the DRGs, but then rose again in 1985. Still, these results must be accepted cautiously, since the changes in coding that occurred with prospective payment mean that the patients in each DRG are not truly comparable in the pre-PPS and PPS eras.

Another sign of how hospitals are changing the services they deliver and the way they deliver them is the decline in the time medicare patients spend in the hospital before undergoing surgery. During this preoperative period, diagnostic tests are performed and the patient is prepared for surgery. The preoperative period had been declining even before prospective payment, as more tests were done on an outpatient

---

*By the same reasoning, if the percentages receiving intensive care drop, or even remain the same, it suggests that patients who would have been admitted to intensive care before prospective payment are not being admitted now.

basis, but the decline between 1983 and 1984 was larger than expected on the basis of past trends. In a sample of more than 700 hospitals, preoperative length of stay for medicare patients dropped from 3.1 days in 1983 to 2.7 days in 1984.[23] It remained at the lower level in 1985.[24]

Other studies based on the CPHA data show that the number of tests and procedures performed during an inpatient stay has also declined under prospective payment.[25] The measures are crude—they show whether particular tests and procedures were done at all during a patient's stay, but not how many times they were done. An analysis of data from 165 hospitals shows that the number of different tests performed, which had been much the same each year from 1980 through 1983, dropped sharply in 1984. The number of drugs per medicare patient was unaffected, rising slightly between 1983 and 1984 in line with the trend from 1980 through 1983.[26]

Using similar data for 137 hospitals over the period 1980–85, Sloan and his colleagues showed that the rate of growth in many tests and procedures dropped much more sharply under prospective payment than did admissions. Medicare admissions in their sample grew 4 percent annually between 1980 and 1983 and declined 4 percent annually between 1983 and 1985, a difference of 8 percent.[27] Thus if the way patients were treated (including their length of stay) remained the same, the growth rates for tests would have turned down by 8 percent as well. Instead, growth rates for most tests dropped much more. For example, the number of patients receiving bone scans, which had grown 6 percent a year before prospective payment, declined 15 percent a year during the first two years of the new payment system. Growth in the number of patients receiving occupational therapy fell from 11 percent a year to −1 percent.

With so much of patients' care moving to other settings—hospital outpatient departments, doctors' offices, nursing homes, and the like—it is important to know whether the decline in inpatient tests and procedures signifies a decline in the total, or just a shift to other settings. Many of the tests and procedures that were once done in the hospital may now be done before or after the hospital stay, as part of the effort to reduce the cost of the stay. None of the studies is able to address this issue. Their data apply only to the inpatient stay and do not show any other care that may have been received by the same patient.

Together with the already declining use of hospitals by people under

TABLE 3-3. The Hospital Industry: Number of Hospitals, Beds, Employees, and Occupancy Rate, Selected Years, 1946–87[a]

Year	Hospitals	Beds (thousands)	Occupancy rate (percent)	Employees[b] (thousands)
1946	4,444	473	72	505
1950	5,031	505	74	662
1955	5,237	568	72	826
1960	5,400	639	75	1,080
1965	5,736	741	76	1,386
1970	5,859	848	78	1,929
1975	5,979	947	75	2,399
1980	5,904	992	75	2,879
1981	5,879	1,007	76	3,039
1982	5,863	1,015	75	3,110
1983	5,843	1,021	73	3,102
1984	5,814	1,020	69	3,023
1985	5,784	1,003	65	3,003
1986	5,728	982	64	3,032
1987	5,659	961	65	3,120

SOURCE: American Hospital Association, *Hospital Statistics,* 1988 ed. (Chicago, 1988), table 1.
a. Nonfederal short-term general and other hospitals ("community" hospitals).
b. Measured in full-time equivalents.

age 65, the decline in use by the elderly induced by prospective payment has brought unprecedented changes to the hospital sector. In 1984 the number of beds in short-stay hospitals declined for the first time in decades and continued to decline through 1987 (table 3-3). The occupancy rate—the average percentage of beds filled with patients during the year—fell from 74 percent in 1983 to 65 percent in 1987. The number of employees dropped slightly in 1983 and more sharply in 1984 and 1985, again for the first time in decades. The industry is faced with a persistent problem of excess inpatient capacity and the need for further cuts.

In response to the new demand for alternatives to inpatient care, hospitals have rapidly added new outpatient facilities and expanded existing ones.[28] In 1986, 63 percent had organized outpatient departments, up from 38 percent in 1982, and the percentage with home health programs had tripled to 35 percent, compared with only 12 percent in 1982. Some of the unused beds were converted for use by long-term, rehabilitation, and other patients not covered under prospective payment. By 1986 the growth in outpatient employment more than offset continued declines in inpatient employment, and total hospital employment turned up once more.

TABLE 3-4. Posthospital Care: Percentages of Medicare Patients Discharged to Various Locations, 1980–85

Location	Before prospective payment				Under prospective payment	
	1980	1981	1982	1983	1984	1985
Home, self-care	84.3	83.6	84.1	82.7	79.4	76.3*
Home, home health care	2.4	2.9	3.2	3.8	5.8*	6.8*
Adjusted percent[a]	...	...	...	...	5.2*	5.6*
Number of patients	672	863	1,011	1,232	1,784	1,983
Skilled-nursing facility	8.2	8.0	7.5	7.8	8.4	9.4*
Adjusted percent[a]	...	...	...	...	7.6	7.8
Number of patients	2,329	2,364	2,343	2,529	2,602	2,750
Intermediate care facility	2.4	2.7	2.4	2.6	2.9	3.5
Other short-term hospital	1.7	1.6	1.6	1.8	1.4	2.3
Discharged against medical advice	0.2	0.3	0.3	0.2	0.2	0.3
Transferred to other facilities	0.8	0.9	0.9	1.1	1.4	1.5
Total admissions (number)	28,471	29,658	31,409	32,587	30,974	29,289

SOURCE: DesHarnais and others, "Impact of the Prospective Payment System," table 2. Percentages are based on a 10 percent sample of discharges in the third quarter of each year from 646 nonfederal short-term general hospitals in states covered by prospective payment.
*Significantly different from trend. Probability is less than .05 that such a large difference from trend could occur by chance.
a. The adjusted percentage is the number of patients discharged to this destination divided by the number of admissions projected to occur in the absence of prospective payment. Projected admissions, from the same source as the other numbers in the table, are 34,056 for 1984 and 35,466 for 1985. Implicit in this adjustment is the assumption that the projected extra patients, those who were not admitted to hospitals under prospective payment but would have been in its absence, would have been discharged to self-care at home.

Posthospital Care

With patients leaving the hospital sooner under prospective payment, it was expected that more of them would be referred to nursing homes and home health services to complete their recovery. Data on the percentages of patients discharged to these facilities are available from the same two studies that reported the use of intensive care.[29] The first study, which covers the years 1980–84, includes 729 hospitals; the second, for 1980–85, includes 646. Again, a 10 percent sample of discharges was drawn from the files of the CPHA for the third quarter of each year. The published percentages are reported in table 3-4, and as with the intensive care data, the most important ones are adjusted for the decline in admissions.

By either measure, the use of home health care rose rapidly under prospective payment. The published figures, 5.8 percent in 1984 and

6.8 percent in 1985, were sharply higher than those of the preceding years (table 3-4). Even after the percentages are recalculated using projected admissions in the absence of prospective payment, they remain well above trend—5.2 percent in 1984 and 5.6 percent in 1985. The use of home health was already increasing, but prospective payment gave it a substantial boost. These findings are buttressed by data on the number of home health agencies. The number of home health agencies certified to participate in the medicare program has grown rapidly since benefits were liberalized in the early 1980s, rising from 2,924 in 1980 to 5,978 in 1986, clearly fast enough to support the shifts that occurred following prospective payment.[30] The agencies increased in size at the same time that they increased in number, averaging 19 employees in 1982 and 30 in 1984, with the additions concentrated in licensed practical nurses, speech pathologists and audiologists, and occupational therapists.[31]

The rise in the published percentages of patients discharged to nursing homes appears to be largely a consequence of the decline in admissions rather than increases in the number of patients referred to nursing homes. The published percentage rose to 9.4 percent by 1985, compared with a little less than 8.0 percent before prospective payment. But when the number of patients sent to nursing homes is divided by the total number of admissions projected to occur in the absence of prospective payment, the percentages fall to 7.6 percent in 1984 and 7.8 percent in 1985, much the same as before prospective payment. The number of patients sent to nursing homes rose modestly in these hospitals between 1983 and 1985, from 2,529 in 1983 to 2,750 in 1985. The primary explanation for the rise in the unadjusted, published percentages was thus the precipitous fall in the denominator, total admissions.

The trends in discharge destination are well established, but it is more difficult to determine what services patients are receiving and how these services have changed. How were hospital and posthospital services combined before prospective payment and how are they being combined now? Within types of posthospital service, such as nursing home care or home health care, have the services provided changed as the use of hospital care has declined? The answers to these questions are important not only because they affect costs but also because it is important to find out how well the new patterns of care serve patients, the question addressed by chapter 4. But answers are hard to come by.

The problem is that no single payer dominates the market for these services the way medicare dominates hospital services for the elderly. Consequently, no payer has a statistical system that can track a representative group of elderly patients from hospitals to nursing homes or home health agencies and finally to the conclusion of their episodes of illness, presenting the full picture of the services received along the way. For nursing homes, individual patients and their families pay the largest portion of expenses out of their own pockets, and no central source records these payments or the services they buy. Medicaid, which helps the poor elderly, is the second-largest payer at about 40 percent of the total. Other payers fill in the remainder; medicare pays less than 2 percent.[32] Medicare is the largest payer for home health care, but still pays less than half the total.[33] Medicaid pays about another quarter and the rest is picked up by various smaller programs and by individuals.

To complicate the situation further, prospective payment was not the only important change affecting nursing homes and home health agencies in the early 1980s. Medicare's home health benefit was made more generous in 1981, as already noted, and helped fuel rapid increases in the use of home health services before prospective payment came along. Many medicaid programs changed their eligibility and payment policies for nursing home care, their largest item of expenditure, in an attempt to curb the growth of program costs.[34] These changes not only altered the incentives facing patients and providers, they may have altered the nature of the patient population covered by the program—for example, when certain groups were dropped from eligibility—making comparisons over time difficult.

The result is that no single source can give a valid statistical picture of the changes that have taken place in posthospital care. No single payer has covered enough patients in a consistent fashion over enough years to permit analyses that can separate prospective payment's effects from those of other changes taking place around the same time. This fact is important to keep in mind because it explains why different studies have come up with different conclusions and why it is difficult to fit these conclusions into a coherent and fully persuasive explanation of what has happened as a result of prospective payment. The best way to make this point is to review briefly the studies that have been done.

NURSING HOMES

It was expected that prospective payment would cause more patients to be referred to nursing homes as care was shifted out of the hospital, and that these patients might well be more acutely ill than those traditionally cared for by nursing homes. The percentages discharged to nursing homes suggest that the number of patients referred from hospitals to nursing homes has not grown much (table 3-4). But shorter hospital stays may mean that different patients are being received, patients who would have completed their recuperation in the hospital before prospective payment, and these patients may need a different type of care. There is some evidence that this has happened. If nursing home patients are sicker but not much more numerous now, the growth of home health may have contributed by siphoning off many of the easier cases.

Perhaps because of the boom in home health, as well as other reasons, there was already a trend toward more sophisticated care in nursing homes before prospective payment, and available studies are not able to disentangle the effects specifically due to prospective payment. A major survey of nursing homes has documented some of the changes.[35] This study surveyed the members of the American Health Care Association and the American Association of Homes for the Aged, two organizations that, between them, include about 90 percent of the roughly 7,000 skilled-nursing facilities certified for participation in medicare or medicaid. Unfortunately, only about 1,400 homes responded to the survey questionnaire. Nonetheless the results are more comprehensive, and less subject to the biases of omission, than those available from any other source.

The survey showed significant increases between 1982 and 1985 in the percentages of patients receiving all but one of the skilled services it asked about (table 3-5), services such as intravenous antibiotics and chemotherapy, catheter care, and rehabilitation services. Other results, not presented here, show rapid increases in the number of nursing homes offering such services. In every case the percentage of homes offering the service is far larger than the percentage of patients receiving it on an average day. For example, in 1985, 46 percent of the homes surveyed could provide intravenous antibiotic therapy when needed, but only 0.9 percent of the patients in these homes received such therapy on an average day. While the survey convincingly shows the increase in skilled services available in nursing homes, it cannot show whether prospective payment affected the trend, since it has data for only two years.

The survey found evidence to support the notion that nursing homes are now caring for more short-stay patients, suggesting that more pa-

TABLE 3-5. Percentages of Patients in Skilled-Nursing Facilities
Receiving Specific Services on an Average Day, 1982 and 1985

Service	1982	1985
Intravenous antibiotic therapy	0.4	0.9*
Intravenous chemotherapy	0.1	0.2*
Total parenteral nutrition	0.1	0.4*
Nasogastric tubes	2.2	4.3*
Inhalation therapy		
Ventilator	0.1	0.2
Oxygen	2.8	4.7*
Tracheostomy	0.5	0.8*
Renal dialysis	0.0	0.1*
Ostomy care	0.0	1.6*
Catheter care	4.3	6.2*
Cardiac rehabilitation	1.0	1.8*
Stroke rehabilitation	4.3	6.7*
Rehabilitation services	10.0	14.3*

SOURCE: Judith Feder, William Scanlon, and Jody Hoffman, "Spillovers from Medicare PPS: Preliminary Results from a Nursing Home Survey," paper presented at the October 1987 meeting of the American Public Health Association, table 4.
*Probability is less than .05 that such a large difference could occur by chance.

tients are using them to recuperate after a hospital stay. The percentage of patients with stays of less than 30 days rose from 24 percent in 1982 to 29 percent in 1985. In addition, in the later year, more patients received the kind of services that indicate an incomplete recovery—swallow therapy for stroke patients, for example, and care for incompletely healed surgical wounds.

A survey of 78 nursing homes in Portland, Oregon, reported evidence suggesting that nursing home patients in that area may require more complex care in the prospective payment era.[36] In April 1985 administrators were asked what changes they had noticed in their patients over the preceding year; two-thirds responded. Eighty percent of them reported that the patients they received were more severely ill. Most of them noted increases in requests for admission on Friday or over the weekend, times when hospitals do few procedures and may try to discharge patients early to cut costs. Many also noted changes in the kinds of patients admitted for care—more patients who were bedridden, who were accompanied by "do-not-resuscitate" orders, and the like, all possible signs that these patients were sicker. The study did not, however, have any information about trends in these problems before prospective payment, and so could not say whether similar changes had occurred in previous years. The author carefully noted that some of the trends might be due to other factors—for ex-

ample, recent changes in the Oregon medicaid program, including an
initiative to encourage the use of home health care in place of nursing
homes, and a growing awareness among nursing home administrators
of the need to have explicit directions about whether to resuscitate
severely ill patients.

The study also collected data on admissions, days in the nursing
home, and deaths for fiscal 1982, 1983, and 1984. The results showed
that deaths per 100,000 days jumped between 1983 and 1984, by an
average of 26 percent. Here, the author was able to show that the average death rate had not changed between 1982 and 1983, making the
later change a more telling indicator that prospective payment may
have played a part by inducing hospitals to discharge sicker patients to
nursing homes.

A study in Wisconsin found a similar phenomenon.[37] The overall
death rate among elderly people in the state was essentially constant
over the period 1980 through 1985, but the *location* of deaths
changed. Throughout the period the percentage of deaths occurring in
hospitals declined, while the percentage occurring in nursing homes
increased. A break in the trend occurred in the last quarter of 1983—
the percentage of deaths in hospitals dropped more sharply than before, and the percentage in nursing homes jumped.

A study of data for all 50 states confirms that prospective payment
has caused a shift toward the use of nursing homes for the terminally
ill.[38] The authors examined the location of death for people aged 65 or
older for the years 1981 through 1985. The proportion dying in nursing homes was essentially constant, at about 19 percent, in 1981,
1982, and 1983. It rose to 20.8 percent in 1984 and further, to 21.5
percent, in 1985. Detailed analysis strongly supported prospective
payment as the cause of the shift: the four states exempt from prospective payment in 1984 showed no evidence of a shift, and the shift was
largest in those states with the largest reductions in length of stay between 1983 and 1984. This finding stands out as one of the clearest
signs that prospective payment has changed the kinds of patients being
received by nursing homes, even if it has not had much effect on their
numbers.

Not all nursing homes, however, report that patients are sicker after
prospective payment than before. A study of nursing homes in southern
California collected data from patients' medical records for three years
(about 2,000 patients in all)—1980, 1982/3, and 1984—in order to

determine whether changes occurring after the start-up of prospective payment were new or the continuation of past trends.[39] Twenty-four nursing homes were included for 1980, 45 for each of the later years. The study looked only at patients being admitted to nursing homes for the first time, not at those who were already institutionalized before their hospital stays. While the ability of the patients to function did change somewhat over the period, the major changes took place between 1980 and 1982/3, before prospective payment; for example, the percentage of patients who were confined to bed rose, and then stayed about the same between 1982/3 and 1984 (changes between 1980 and 1982/3 may have been influenced by the change in the number of homes surveyed). The percentage who were continent declined between 1980 and 1982/3, and again, by a smaller amount, between 1982/3 and 1984. Reviewing their results, the authors concluded that the types of patients admitted did not change much and noted that "had it not been for the 1982/3 sample, it would have been convenient to attribute changes between the 1980 and 1984 cohorts to the PPS." [40]

A study of 10 nursing homes in Georgia, which looked at two periods, one before and one after the implementation of prospective payment, also failed to find evidence that patients admitted in the later year were sicker than those admitted earlier.[41] Data were collected from the medical records of a small sample of patients (353 in all) in the second half of 1982 and again in the second half of 1984. Changes occurred in both directions. While the percentage of patients who were incontinent increased, as did the percentage with nasogastric tubes, the percentages dying or readmitted to hospitals within a month of admission fell.

Other studies pertinent to the issue suffer from greater difficulties than the ones already cited. Neu and Harrison, for example, looked at nursing home and home health care in 1981 and again in 1984/5, thus leaving them no way to know whether the changes they observed took place before prospective payment or under it.[42] Further, since they studied the care *paid for by medicare,* their results were influenced not only by changes in the patterns of care but also by changes in the amounts of that care for which medicare agreed to pay. They suggest that the increase in short nursing home stays observed between 1981 and 1984/5 reflected less-sick patients, but it might also reflect more patients recuperating after a hospital stay (and these are not necessarily less sick), or even more restrictive benefit payments.[43]

TABLE 3-6. Home Health Care Services Paid for by Medicare,
1974–86

Year[a]	Persons served (thousands)	Persons served per 1,000 enrollees	Visits per person served
1974	393	16	21
1976	589	23	23
1978	770	28	23
1980	957	34	23
1982	1,172	40	26
1983	1,351	45	27
1984	1,516	50	27
1985	1,587	51	25
1986	1,600	50	24

SOURCE: Martin Ruther and Charles Helbing, "Use and Cost of Home Health Agency Services under Medicare," *Health Care Financing Review,* vol. 10 (Fall 1988), table 1.
a. Year service was received. Numbers include disabled beneficiaries.

HOME HEALTH

For home health, as for nursing homes, the expectation was that prospective payment would produce more patients, and more seriously ill patients. The data already presented on percentages discharged to home health show that the number of patients has indeed increased. Whether these patients are sicker is another matter— shorter hospital stays suggest they may be, but the larger number of patients suggests that at least some are using home health who did not use it before, and they may be less sick. In addition, still other patients may use home health care even though they were not referred to it by the hospital, especially since a hospital stay is no longer required to qualify for medicare coverage.

Statistics on the numbers of people and visits covered by medicare show persons served per 1,000 enrollees rising rapidly from the mid-1970s until 1984, and then leveling off (table 3-6). Visits per person served rose more slowly, but also leveled off in 1984, and began to drop. The leveling-off may have more to do with medicare's coverage decisions than with the need for, or use of, home health services. In recent years, there have been accusations that medicare is interpreting the benefit in a more restrictive way, leading to a sharp increase in the number of payment denials and a slowing in the rate of growth of home health services.[44]

More comprehensive data covering all care, no matter who pays for it, are unavailable. Anecdotal and survey evidence suggests that the number of home health services probably increased substantially during the period following prospective payment, a trend more in line with expectations. A survey answered by 90 Area Agencies on Aging found large increases in services between the year before and the year following the implementation of prospective payment in each area.* Case management services increased 365 percent, skilled nursing provided in the patient's home almost 200 percent, and housekeeping and personal care services both increased more than 60 percent. The survey is described as random and the agencies are described as widely distributed geographically, but no information is given about their distribution, so it is unclear whether they can be considered representative of the nation.

Physicians' Services and Outpatient Surgery

One way to get an overview of the changes that have been taking place in the medical care of elderly people is to look at where physicians deliver their services, as reflected in the bills submitted to medicare (table 3-7). Charges for services delivered to patients in the hospital fell from 61 percent of the total in 1982 to 47 percent in 1986, while charges for services rendered in the outpatient departments of hospitals were up strongly, and those for services in doctors' offices and other settings were up moderately.

The changes are particularly concentrated in surgical services, and here the timing is closely linked to the start of prospective payment. Between 1983 and 1984 the share of surgical charges paid for surgery on inpatients fell from almost 80 percent to 74 percent, and continued to fall in later years, to 57 percent by 1986. At the same time, charges paid for surgery in hospital outpatient departments rose from 6.6 percent of the total in 1983 to 26.3 percent in 1986. The share of charges for office surgery rose more modestly, from 13 percent in 1983 to about 16 percent. Thus the most dramatic shift revealed by these statistics is from inpatient to outpatient surgery.

Thanks in part to technological advances in lens procedures, particularly in cataract surgery, that have made outpatient surgery feasible and safe, ophthalmology has contributed more to this shift than any other specialty.[45] In 1985 ophthalmologists were responsible for almost 20 percent of all surgical charges submitted to medicare, a share

---

*Funded by federal money that comes to them through the state, Area Agencies on Aging are responsible for planning, coordinating, and advocating services for the elderly. Usually, they do not provide services themselves but subcontract with providers to do so.

TABLE 3-7. Distribution of Doctors' Charges Paid by Medicare for Services Performed in Various Settings, 1982–86[a]

Year and place of service	All services	Surgical services
1982		
Total charges (millions of dollars)	15,000	4,900
Distribution (percentages):		
Office	29.7	12.5
Inpatient hospital	60.8	82.0
Outpatient hospital	4.7	4.9
Other	4.8	0.6
1983		
Total charges (millions of dollars)	17,400	5,800
Distribution (percentages):		
Office	29.7	13.0
Inpatient hospital	60.0	79.8
Outpatient hospital	5.4	6.6
Other	4.9	0.6
1984		
Total charges (millions of dollars)	19,200	6,500
Distribution (percentages):		
Office	29.9	13.6
Inpatient hospital	56.5	74.2
Outpatient hospital	8.3	11.3
Other	5.3	0.9
1985		
Total charges (millions of dollars)	20,800	7,100
Distribution (percentages):		
Office	32.1	16.1
Inpatient hospital	49.7	63.0
Outpatient hospital	12.1	19.9
Other	6.1	0.9
1986		
Total charges (millions of dollars)	22,900[b]	8,000
Distribution (percentages):		
Office	31.4	15.5
Inpatient hospital	47.0	57.0
Outpatient hospital	15.7	26.3
Other	5.9	1.2

SOURCES: For 1982–85 data: Charles R. Fisher, "Impact of the Prospective Payment System on Physician Charges under Medicare," *Health Care Financing Review,* vol. 8 (Summer 1987), tables 1, 2. For 1986 data: Charles R. Fisher, "Trends in Medicare Enrollee Use of Physician and Supplier Services, 1983–86," *Health Care Financing Review,* vol. 10 (Fall 1988), table 12.

a. Charges are the medicare "allowed" charges, that is, the amounts medicare agrees to pay; the physician's actual charge may be larger.

b. The sum of all services except "Other."

matched only by general surgeons. Although all surgical specialties showed some movement toward outpatient settings between 1980 and 1985, the shift was by far the largest in ophthalmology. In 1980 ophthalmologists billed 87 percent of their surgical charges for procedures performed on inpatients. By 1985 inpatient surgery had dropped to only 25 percent of their billings. Ophthalmology has become the bread-and-butter of hospital outpatient departments, accounting for more than half of their surgical charges for medicare patients.

Prospective rates provide no incentives to do outpatient surgery, which completely replaces a hospital stay, but the Peer Review Organizations do, through their review of hospital admissions. As noted earlier, they review certain types of cases before they are admitted to the hospital with the aim of recommending outpatient surgery whenever it is possible, and they deny payment for admissions judged to be unnecessary, which encourages doctors and hospitals to consider outpatient care. Often doctors turn to outpatient care without applying for permission to admit patients because they expect it to be denied.[46] Lens procedures were given special attention by most PROs. The liberalization in 1982 of benefits for outpatient surgery performed in hospitals and freestanding surgery centers, and medicare's continuation of cost reimbursement for hospital outpatient care until October 1, 1987, also encouraged its use. One study reports that hospitals probably received more for cataract surgery done in outpatient departments than for the same procedure performed on inpatients.[47]

More detailed documentation of what has happened is, however, hampered by problems similar to those that plague the study of post-hospital care. There are three main settings for outpatient surgery—hospitals, freestanding centers, and doctors' offices. No single data source provides comprehensive information about all three of them. The most plentiful information is available for outpatient surgery performed in hospitals, much less for freestanding centers and doctors' offices.

Outpatient surgery performed in hospitals, for patients of all ages, has grown enormously in a very short time. These procedures totaled 8.7 million in 1986, 40 percent of all surgical procedures performed in hospitals,[48] a percentage that some have suggested is the upper limit on what is possible in outpatient settings.[49] As recently as 1981 outpatient procedures accounted for less than 20 percent of the surgery done in hospitals.[50] Freestanding centers performed another million outpatient surgical procedures in 1986.[51]

Two pieces of evidence shed more light on surgery for medicare patients in hospital outpatient departments, and the possible role of prospective payment. One study, cited earlier, found over half the decline in medicare admissions between the third quarter of 1983 and the third quarter of 1984 in the study hospitals could be attributed to the shift of lens procedures to outpatient settings.[52] Another study found that medicare admissions in 40 DRGs for which outpatient surgery was a definite possibility rose from 1980 through 1983 and then fell 15 percent between 1983 and 1984 in the nearly 700 hospitals included in the study.[53] The authors pursued the issue by studying the same DRGs in 49 hospitals that reported inpatient and outpatient surgery for 1984 and 1985. Medicare admissions in these DRGs continued to fall in the two years, while outpatient surgical procedures grew more than enough to compensate: inpatient admissions fell from 21,000 to 17,000, while outpatient procedures grew from 8,000 to 13,000, making them 44 percent of all the surgery performed on medicare patients in these hospitals. Non-medicare admissions in the same DRGs fell throughout the period, in both samples of hospitals, and the increase in outpatient surgery for non-medicare patients between 1984 and 1985 was even greater than that for medicare patients, suggesting that the medicare trends are at least partly the consequence of forces that go well beyond prospective payment and its review mechanisms.

Recent changes in medicare may contribute to a tempering of the trend.[54] Services provided in hospital outpatient departments continued to be reimbursed on the basis of costs after the introduction of prospective payment for inpatient care, but expenditures for these services rose so rapidly that Congress ordered limits on payment, beginning in October 1987. Under these provisions, all surgery performed in outpatient departments will be subject to prospectively set rates by the end of 1989, as is already the case for surgery done in freestanding centers. In addition, outpatient surgery will be reviewed by PROs under the new contracts they sign with the Department of Health and Human Services, and beneficiaries are once again responsible for deductibles and coinsurance for outpatient surgery.

CHAPTER FOUR

Effects on the Health of the Elderly

A CRUCIAL issue for prospective payment is its effects on the health of the elderly. Prospective rates create strong incentives for hospitals to cut costs in order to stay in business and make a profit; if this cost cutting takes the form of omitting services important to patients' health, some elderly people may suffer from poorer health or greater disability than necessary. Some may even die. Further, if the rates are not increased by enough each year to allow hospitals to provide the newest and best technologies, the health of the elderly in the future may not improve as rapidly as would be desirable.

Senator John Heinz expressed some of these concerns in a statement that opened hearings by the Senate's Special Committee on Aging in 1985: "From the beginning, this committee has been concerned that DRGs make older Americans on Medicare potential victims of poor quality care. Specifically, I have expressed concern on several previous occasions that hospitals might attempt to hedge the system through premature discharges or inappropriate transfers of patients. I have also warned that the watchdog Peer Review Organizations, the PRO's, might be tied to the fence on a short leash when it comes to quality oversight and enforcement."[1] The senator was referring to widely shared worries that shorter stays might mean that patients were discharged before they were well enough, and that hospitals might try to transfer severely ill patients to other institutions rather than lose money on them.

What effects has prospective payment had on the health of the elderly? Without question, elderly patients are being cared for differently now, with shorter hospital stays and more posthospital care. Have these changes come about solely through improved efficiency, or have they made a difference, good or bad, in the outcomes for patients? If so, how much of a difference? Before the nation can decide whether the benefits of prospective payment are worth its costs, it must know what those costs are, and the most important possible cost is a decline in the quality of care. This chapter discusses what is known about the effects of prospective payment on patients' health.

So far, what is known is that there have been no unusual changes in the death rate of the elderly, an extreme outcome but an important indicator of serious quality problems. Nor has there been any clear deterioration in other, indirect signs of quality, such as readmissions. Premature discharges have been an occasional problem, but have not turned out to be as widespread as feared. Beyond that, although problems have been suggested by a few small studies done in individual hospitals, there is not much in the way of systematic evidence about quality—almost nothing on outcomes short of death. Indeed, the lack of systematic evidence is one of the most important points about this issue. Not much was known about quality before prospective payment and not much is known now, not nearly enough to feel confident in drawing firm conclusions. The issue deserves close attention, and better data, in the years to come.

The Peer Review Organizations (PROs) were, as Senator Heinz put it, created to serve as watchdogs for the new payment system. Since they first started work, in 1984, their responsibilities for monitoring the quality of care have been expanded substantially by Congress in response to reports of problems. Not much of what the PROs have discovered has yet been made public. Equally if not more important for purposes of evaluating the quality of care given the elderly, the PROs' investigations suffer from the lack of any comparable information from the period before prospective payment. They will be able to document changes in quality in the future, but not to show whether changes in quality have already occurred that can be attributed to prospective payment.

The rest of the chapter considers the quality of care under prospective payment and the mechanisms for monitoring it. Mortality rates are presented first, then other measures. The responsibilities of PROs for monitoring quality are described in some detail. The last section of the chapter suggests how prospective payment may affect medical care over the longer term.

Mortality of the Elderly under Prospective Payment

The death rate of the elderly population—deaths per 100,000 people aged 65 and older—has not shown any clear trend since the

FIGURE 4-1. Deaths per 100,000 Population Aged 65 or Older, 1970–86

Deaths per 100,000 population

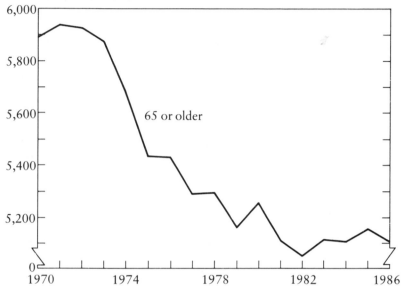

SOURCE: Data supplied by the National Center for Health Statistics.

beginning of prospective payment (figure 4-1). For most of the 1970s, it dropped fairly steadily, often precipitously, from almost 6,000 deaths per 100,000 people each year to about 5,200. Since 1979 there has been little further progress; the rate has gone up nearly as often as it has gone down.* The fluctuations since 1983—a slight decline between 1983 and 1984, a somewhat larger rise between 1984 and 1985, and a return in 1986 to the level of 1984—are within the bounds set by recent experience. A very close reading of the data suggests that the changes since 1982 might be the start of an upward trend, a trend that could be attributed to payment changes if the cost limits under the Tax Equity and Fiscal Responsibility Act of 1982 (TEFRA) affected the quality of care even before prospective payment

* When the death rate is adjusted for the growing number of very old people, the story is the same—rapid improvement until 1979 and little or no progress since. See Health Care Financing Administration, Office of Research and Demonstrations, *Report to Congress: Impact of the Medicare Hospital Prospective Payment System, 1985 Annual Report*, HCFA Pub. 03251 (Baltimore: U.S. Department of Health and Human Services, August 1987), p. 4.51a, table 4-29.

FIGURE 4-2. Death Rates of the Elderly, by 10-Year Age-Group, 1970–86

Deaths per 100,000 population

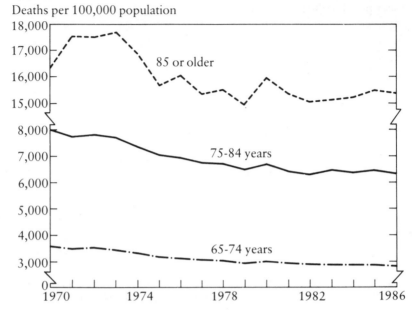

SOURCES: For 1980–86: Data supplied by the National Center for Health Statistics. For 1970–80: *Vital Statistics of the United States, 1980*, vol. 2: *Mortality*, pt. A, DHHS Pub. (PHS) 85-110 (Washington: National Center for Health Statistics, 1985), p. 3, table 1-3.

got under way. But until several more years of data are available, it will be impossible to tell whether this is the case.

Death rates for the elderly by 10-year age-groups strengthen the impression made by the overall rate (figure 4-2). Only the rate for the very old, those 85 or older, shows a definite upturn in the 1980s. The rate increased from 1982 to 1985 before turning down in 1986, but the entire increase over the period is less than the single-year jump between 1979 and 1980. And again, the timing fails to point clearly to prospective payment as a possible cause, since the upturn began in 1982. Further experience must accumulate before it becomes clear whether this is truly a new trend.[2]

These death rates, which measure all deaths of elderly people, include too much, however, to be good, precise tests of the impact of prospective payment. They reflect not only medical care, but everything and anything else that influences the health of the elderly, including changes over time in such important habits as smoking, exercise, and diet. Rates that focus on deaths in the hospital, or deaths following a hospitalization, are more likely to reflect any changes brought about by prospective payment.

Of two common measures of this type, discharge mortality—the percentage of hospital stays that end in death—is a poor measure under the special circumstances created by prospective payment. The principal problem is the same one that afflicted measures of intensive care and posthospital care in the last chapter: discharge mortality is expressed as a percentage of admissions, and admissions have declined. Thus even if the same number of people die in the hospital as before prospective payment, the discharge mortality rate would go up simply because of the decline in admissions. The number of deaths counted as hospital deaths might also be affected by prospective payment. For example, the number of hospital deaths would decline if some terminally ill patients, who would have been allowed to die in the hospital before prospective payment even though little or nothing could be done to help them, are now sent to nursing homes or hospices, or even cared for at home in their last days. Several studies suggest that shifts of this kind are taking place.[3] Thus it is not at all clear what to make of the fact that discharge mortality has been essentially unchanged under prospective payment: the Commission on Professional and Hospital Activities found that it was between 6 and 7 percent in 1984 and 1985, just as it had been before prospective payment.[4]

A much better measure is the number of deaths within six weeks of a hospital admission, per 1,000 elderly medicare enrollees. Elderly enrollees are the population at risk of suffering from any deterioration in quality, and their number is unaffected by changes in the pattern of care. And the count of deaths is not biased by changes in the place of death because the death is counted regardless of where it occurs, as long as it occurs within six weeks of the time the patient was admitted to a hospital. Indeed, since six weeks includes part of the posthospital period for most patients, this rate reflects the combined effects of hospital care and whatever other care the patient received after discharge from the hospital. It does, however, exclude the deaths of patients who would have been admitted to a hospital before prospective payment but who are now treated in other settings.

This rate, deaths within six weeks of admission to a hospital per 1,000 elderly medicare enrollees, has fluctuated around a stable level during the 1980s, and showed no departure from this level in 1984, the only year of prospective payment for which data are currently

TABLE 4-1. Deaths within Six Weeks of Hospital Admission, per 1,000 Elderly Medicare Enrollees, 1980–84[a]

Year	Deaths per 1,000	Year	Deaths per 1,000
1980	29.2	1983	30.3
1981	28.5	1984[b]	29.3
1982	29.7		

SOURCES: Health Care Financing Administration, Office of Research and Demonstrations, *Report to Congress: Impact of the Medicare Hospital Prospective Payment System, 1985 Annual Report*, HCFA Pub. 03251 (Baltimore: U.S. Department of Health and Human Services, August 1987), page 4.67a.
   a.   In prospective payment states. In the states exempt from prospective payment, this rate rose from 27.5 in 1980 to 29.1 in 1984.
   b.   Fiscal 1984 (October 1, 1983, to October 1, 1984).

available (table 4-1). In states under prospective payment, the rate was 29.3 in 1984, the lowest since 1981. Nothing about the rate suggests serious quality problems in the first year of prospective payment.

Other Measures of Quality

While a sharp rise in the death rate would be a cause for concern, the lack of one is not fully reassuring. A report by the Department of Health and Human Services notes that "poor quality of care could result in increased disability, discomfort, or hardship without having a measurable effect on mortality. Thus the absence of a measurable change in mortality does not necessarily mean that there has been no change in the quality of care."[5] Good measures of outcomes short of death are not readily available, but some clues can be gleaned from indirect measures, such as readmission and transfer rates, and from the few studies that have examined medical records for evidence of such problems as premature discharges.

In the first year of prospective payment, cases of premature discharge—discharge from the hospital before the patient is sufficiently recovered to be safely sent home, or to another institution—were reported to Congress by constituents.[6] The predecessors of the PROs, the similarly named Professional Standards Review Organizations, who filled in until the PROs were signed up (and who usually won the PRO contracts), reported finding cases of early discharge in their review of medical records.[7] Because premature discharge is clearly a danger to the patient and can lead to readmissions that would otherwise be unnecessary and thus to extra expense for the medicare program, one of the specific jobs required of Peer Review Organizations during their first two years was the detection and prevention of premature discharges.

The inspector general of the Department of Health and Human Services studied a sample of more than 7,000 medicare hospital admissions to check for premature discharges, among other problems.[8] The admissions took place between October 1984 and March 1985, the first six months of prospective payment's second year and the first period during which all eligible hospitals were included. Based on reviews of the patients' medical records, the study concluded that less than 1 percent, 0.8 percent, were discharged prematurely. Most of the premature discharges occurred in small, rural, nonteaching hospitals and may have been part of a more general problem of quality in these hospitals—the study reported that most cases of premature discharge involved other quality problems. The inspector general's report noted that the number of premature discharges it found were "fewer than previously suspected" and that, since the time the sample was drawn, the PROs had been given increased powers to deal with such cases, including the authority to deny payment for a readmission associated with an earlier premature discharge.*

Readmission to the hospital shortly after discharge may also indicate that care during the first stay was deficient in some way—not only because the patient might have been discharged too early, but because incomplete or inept treatment during the first stay led to a relapse. To guard against this problem, the PROs were directed during their first two years to investigate all readmissions within seven days of a discharge; during their second two years, the period was increased to 15 days.[9] With the third round of contracts, PROs have been asked to review a sample of readmissions within 31 days.

Whether because of their deficiencies or in spite of them, readmission statistics do not reveal any clear signs of deterioration in quality (table 4-2). Readmissions within 30 and 60 days, as calculated from medicare's files of admissions completed within the year, show the readmission rate rising to a higher level in 1982 but remaining at that level, essentially unchanged, through the first two years of prospective payment. Readmissions within the third quarter of each year, based on

---

* Note, however, that with this as with many other possible measures of quality, there is no information about the situation before prospective payment. Some premature discharges may have occurred before prospective payment, presumably not because of payment incentives, but as a result of poor care and poor decisions about care by physicians or hospital staff.

TABLE 4-2. Percentage of Elderly Medicare Patients Readmitted to the Hospital within Various Periods, 1979–85

Year	Department of Health and Human Services[a]		Commission on Professional and Hospital Activities[b]
	30 days	60 days	Same quarter
1979	16.2	22.7	...
1980	15.6	21.8	12.2
1981	16.1	22.5	12.6
1982	17.9	24.5	12.7
1983	17.7	24.3	13.2
1984	17.8[c]	24.5[c]	14.0
1985	18.0[c]	...	14.1

SOURCES: HCFA, *1985 Impact Report*, Pub. 03251, p. 4.72a, 4.73a; HCFA, Office of Research and Demonstrations, *Report to Congress: The Impact of the Medicare Hospital Prospective Payment System, 1986 Annual Report,* HCFA Pub. 03281 (Baltimore: Department of Health and Human Services, June 1989), p. 4.31a, table 4.18; and Susan DesHarnais, James Chesney, and Steven Fleming, "The Impact of the Prospective Payment System on Hospital Utilization and the Quality of Care: Trends and Regional Variations in the First Two Years," paper presented at the October 1987 meeting of the American Public Health Association, table 3.

a. The Department of Health and Human Services includes any readmission during the year that occurs within 30 (or 60) days of an initial admission, counting from the first day of the initial admission. The medicare file for 1984 is somewhat less complete than the files for earlier years, which could lead to an undercount of admissions and readmissions in that year.

b. The Commission on Professional and Hospital Activities counts only admissions and readmissions that are completed within the third quarter of each year, but does not limit the length of time between them.

c. Fiscal years. The federal fiscal year begins on October 1 of the preceding calendar year.

cases reported to the Commission on Professional and Hospital Activities for which both admissions were completed within the quarter, rose throughout 1980–85; the rise between 1983 and 1984 is the largest, but this could simply reflect the sharp drop in admissions, and, even so, the increase is not out of line with the trend.*

Like readmissions, transfers to another hospital are a possible sign of trouble. Under prospective payment, the first hospital receives a payment for each day the patient spent there, while the second hospital receives the full rate for that DRG.[10] If the second hospital is not under prospective payment, as rehabilitation, long-term care, and psychiatric hospitals are not, it is paid its actual costs, subject to a limit on the increase in costs from year to year. Thus a hospital might choose to transfer a costly patient for financial reasons, even if the transfer were not in the best interests of the patient.

Studies by the Commission on Professional and Hospital Activities

* Smaller studies can often examine issues in more detail, but their findings may reflect special circumstances rather than general trends. One study of a single hospital examined the readmission rate for patients with congestive heart failure and found that it declined substantially after prospective payment. See Michael W. Rich and Kenneth E. Freedland, "Effect of DRGs on Three-Month Readmission Rate of Geriatric Patients with Congestive Heart Failure," *American Journal of Public Health,* vol. 78 (June 1988), pp. 680–82.

TABLE 4-3. Number and Percentage of Medicare Patients
Transferred to Other Hospitals, 1980–85

	Before prospective payment				Under prospective payment	
Transferred to:	1980	1981	1982	1983	1984	1985
Other short-term hospitals						
Number	493	475	515	586	427	665
Percent	1.7	1.6	1.6	1.8	1.4	2.3
Adjusted percent[a]	...	...	...	...	1.3	1.9
Other facilities						
Number	233	276	286	358	427	451
Percent[a]	0.8	0.9	0.9	1.1	1.4	1.5
Adjusted percent[a]	...	...	...	...	1.3	1.3
Total admissions[b]	28,471	29,658	31,409	32,587	30,974	29,289

SOURCE: DesHarnais and others, "Impact of the Prospective Payment System," tables 2, 3.
  a. The adjusted percentage is the number of transfers divided by the number of admissions projected to occur in the absence of prospective payment. Projected admissions are 34,056 for 1984 and 35,466 for 1985 and are taken from the same source.
  b. Figures are based on a 10 percent sample of discharges in the third quarter of each year from 646 nonfederal short-term general hospitals in states covered by prospective payment. The authors report that none of the percentages for the period of prospective payment are statistically different from the trend established between 1980 and 1983.

show that the percentage of patients transferred to other short-term
hospitals dropped in 1984, but the percentage transferred to other facilities, those not likely to be included in prospective payment, increased significantly even after the figure was adjusted for the decline
in admissions (these results, not shown here, are based on third-
quarter admissions to 729 hospitals for each year, 1980–84).[11] When
the sample was examined the next year—the number of hospitals now
down to 646 because of the requirement for six complete years of
data—transfers to short-term hospitals again showed a drop in 1984,
but this was followed by a sharp rise in 1985 (table 4-3). Transfers to
other facilities showed increases in both years. While the trend was
clearly upward for both kinds of transfers, the percentages in this
sample, adjusted and unadjusted for the drop in admissions, were not
significantly different by statistical test from past years.

Transfers may not be the only way hospitals avoid expensive patients. Another study based on CPHA data found that, while the increase in the transfer rate under prospective payment was in line with
earlier trends, admissions of medicare patients who first appeared in
the emergency room increased significantly after 1983.[12] The authors
speculated that hospitals might avoid some patients by not admitting
them at all, instead rendering emergency treatment and sending them

TABLE 4-4. Admissions per 1,000 Elderly Medicare Enrollees, by Age, Sex, and Race, 1980–85[a]

Type of enrollee	1980	1983	1984[b]	1985[b]	Average annual percent change		
					1980–83	1983–84	1984–85
All	380	403	393	355	2.0	− 3.5	− 9.6
Aged:							
65–69	294	302	289	256	0.8	− 5.7	− 11.1
70–74	353	374	362	327	1.9	− 4.0	− 9.8
75–79	424	453	442	398	2.2	− 3.2	− 9.9
80–84	487	526	514	469	2.6	− 2.9	− 8.8
85 and older	532	569	564	521	2.3	− 1.2	− 7.6
Male	409	428	415	382	1.5	− 3.9	− 8.0
Female	361	387	377	337	2.4	− 3.2	− 10.7
White	387	409	398	358	1.9	− 3.6	− 9.9
Other	331	363	356	332	3.1	− 2.5	− 6.8

SOURCE: HCFA, 1986 Impact Report, Pub. 03281, p. 4.7a, table 4.3.
  a. Includes only enrollees in states under prospective payment.
  b. Fiscal years. The federal fiscal year begins on October 1 of the preceding calendar year.

to another hospital; there was, however, no evidence that patients admitted through the emergency room were sicker than average, and therefore likely to be costlier. Or it might be that the stricter criteria for admission under prospective payment mean that more patients suffer symptoms that send them to the emergency room. The authors concluded that the finding deserved further investigation.

Even when statistics for the elderly population as a whole show no problems, subgroups may be experiencing difficulties. It has been a matter of concern that the most vulnerable subgroups, the very old and minorities, for example, might have problems under prospective payment that do not show up in aggregate numbers. One way to check on this possibility is to examine the changes in admissions and length of stay for these subgroups and compare them with the rest of the elderly, to see whether they have taken the brunt of the cuts.

Admissions per 1,000 medicare enrollees, by age, sex, and race, are reassuring on this score (table 4-4). They show that the rate of admissions dropped the most for the youngest and presumably healthiest enrollees, those aged 65 to 69 years old, and the least for the very old, those 85 and older. Similarly, the admission rate dropped more for white enrollees than for those of other races. Length of stay followed the opposite pattern in 1984 and 1985—stays dropped the most for the very old and for other races.[13] While, for the very old, this simply continued the trend established before prospective payment, when length of stay also fell more for those aged 85 and older than for younger enrollees, it raises the possibility that premature discharges may be a particular problem for this group.*[14]

In contrast to the pattern of services discussed in the last chapter, and despite a few indications of possible trouble spots, none of the data on quality show clear and major changes. None point unequivocally to deterioration (or improvement) in the quality of care. The measures available are, however, fairly blunt instruments. Death rates will pick up only the most serious quality problems, while the other measures—readmissions and the like—are highly indirect ways to get at the real question: how are patients doing?

The Peer Review Organizations are addressing this question more directly with their reviews of patients' medical records. The details of this review are described later in the chapter, but the point here is that a large amount of information on the quality of care, at least in hospitals, has been accumulated and is potentially available, although most of it has not been made public. On the basis of this information, the president of the American Medical Peer Review Association, the association of PROs, testified before Congress that "the PRO community has, to date, been all but unanimous in stating that quality of inpatient care has not declined as a result of this new payment approach. In fact, in a survey of AMPRA's membership conducted last spring, many respondents noted that quality of hospital care had improved."[15]

This huge fund of information is subject to major shortcomings, shortcomings that make it difficult to know how the PROs were able to reach their conclusions. The most critical for drawing conclusions about the impact of prospective payment is that little in the way of quality review was done by the PROs' predecessor organizations, and no common methodology was used for what was done—there is no comparable fund of information with which to compare the PROs' findings. In fact, a common approach for reviewing quality was not introduced until the third year of prospective payment, so that differences in methods may cloud the results for the first two years.

Further, even now, quality review pertains almost entirely to hospital inpatient care—little is known about the quality of posthospital

* Or it may just be that lengths of stay dropped the most for these groups exactly because their admissions dropped less than average. The decline in length of stay thus was not offset by the loss of many shorter-stay patients to the same extent that it was in other subgroups.

and outpatient care, before or after the introduction of prospective payment. With the increasing use of these services, the assessment of their quality becomes increasingly important. And more important than the assessment of individual services—hospital, nursing home, home health, and outpatient—is the assessment of the whole. The crucial question is how well the *combination* of services works for the patient rather than how well each works alone: what is the final outcome for the patient, and how does that compare with the outcomes from other possible combinations of services? As many of those directly concerned with measuring quality have stressed, when the focus is on the ultimate outcome—the patient's health when an episode of illness is over—the review should examine the services provided during the whole episode and their cumulative effect, not particular types of services in isolation.[16]

It is not too late, although it would be difficult, expensive, and time-consuming, to do some careful before-and-after studies based on patients' medical records. The records in most hospitals are adequate for such studies. Those in other facilities, and especially in doctors' offices, are likely to present greater problems.[17] But the hardest part would be linking patients' records across facilities. The kinds of data available from medicare's files, although considerably easier to link, cannot do the job. They do not include enough information to allow patients to be matched for condition before and after prospective payment, nor do they include the outcome information that is essential for direct conclusions about the quality of care delivered.

The two studies of elderly hip fracture patients already cited in chapter 3 demonstrate the value of research based on medical records.[18] In both studies the authors excluded patients who were in a hospital or institution at the time of the fracture, who had had hip fractures before, or for whom cancer contributed to the fracture. The point of this painstaking selection—possible only with the kind of data available from medical records—was to ensure that the patients were similar, so that any differences in outcome could be attributed to differences in treatment rather than in their initial condition. The earlier study, done in a teaching hospital, compared 47 patients for the years 1981–83 with 23 for the years 1984–85, when the hospital came under prospective payment. The later one, drawing on the records of a large community hospital, had 149 patients for the period before prospective payment (October 1981 through December

1983) and 189 prospective payment patients (January 1984 to March 1, 1986).

What stands out from both studies is that, after prospective payment, a far higher percentage of the patients were discharged to nursing homes *and were still there six months or a year after leaving the hospital.* In the first study, 13 percent of the patients hospitalized during 1981–83 were in nursing homes after six months; 39 percent of the patients hospitalized during 1984–85 were. In the second study, which followed patients for a full year after discharge from the hospital, 9 percent of those hospitalized during 1981–83 were still in a nursing home a year later, compared with 33 percent of those hospitalized under prospective payment. Although institutionalization is not a direct measure of the patients' ability to function, these rates clearly indicate that many more of the patients in the later period could not get around on their own well enough to be discharged.

The authors focused on physical therapy as the most likely explanation for the change, but their findings failed to show that this was consistently the problem. In both studies, length of stay dropped sharply with the advent of prospective payment. In the first study, the use of physical therapy dropped sharply as well, from an average of 9.7 sessions to 4.9 sessions. But in the second, doctors apparently compensated for the shorter stays by ordering therapy at more frequent intervals, so that the average declined only moderately, from 7.6 to 6.3 sessions; nonetheless, the shorter period for recuperation meant that fewer patients were able to walk at the time of their discharge from the hospital—40 percent as compared with 56 percent before prospective payment. In both studies, those who were sent to a nursing home and remained there were disproportionately those without help at home.

If the results had ended there, the findings would appear to provide clear evidence of a decline in the quality of care because of prospective payment. The second, larger study, however, offered an intriguing alternative explanation. In that study, 20 percent of the patients under prospective payment belonged to a health maintenance organization (HMO), which received a fixed annual payment for each enrollee to cover all costs of care (no one had been enrolled in an HMO before prospective payment). There were no discernible differences between these patients and the others in their personal characteristics or their fractures. The HMO patients had even shorter stays and fewer physical therapy sessions in the hospital and were more likely to be discharged to a nursing home (83 percent versus 55 percent of the other patients). *Yet a year later only 16 percent of the HMO patients were still in nursing homes, compared with 35 percent of the other patients.* For the HMO patients, the ultimate outcome under prospective payment was much closer to the outcomes for all patients before prospective payment.

This finding suggests that something about the way the HMO managed the care of its patients differed considerably from the way the rest of the patients were managed. Further, it suggests that the poorer outcomes experienced by the other patients were not a necessary consequence of prospective payment. Where prospective payment leads to poorer care, it may thus be possible to make other changes to offset the decline rather than either accepting it as unavoidable, or, alternatively, abandoning prospective payment.

Findings like these are far more illuminating and raise more troubling, and more useful, questions than small changes in, say, the readmission rate. Those small changes are potentially useful as a first cut at detecting quality changes but are too limited to be more than that. To find out more about what prospective payment means for care, more studies like the hip fracture studies must be done.[19] In the meantime, the facts about quality will remain scant and difficult to interpret. As one observer has noted, "In terms of quality, there is no documented trend toward a reduction in quality of health care under PPS. By the same token, though, there are no routine data analyses of morbidity, mortality, and consumer satisfaction comparable to those currently done for use and expenditures on which to base an assessment of quality."[20]

The Peer Review Organizations (PROs)*

Because the Peer Review Organizations are deeply involved, and increasingly so, in assessing the quality of care, they occupy a strategic position in the debate over this issue. They have the potential to be valuable sources of information for the long-term assessment of prospective payment's costs and benefits and, more generally, the costs and benefits of medical care in the United States. How they monitor the quality of care, and how successfully, are thus matters of considerable importance.

* This section was co-authored with Carrie Lynn Manning.

The PROs were created by Congress, in the 1982 legislation that called for prospective payment, because of fears that the new system would be subject to abuses of the sort that have been mentioned in chapter 3 and this chapter—unnecessary admissions, premature discharges, excessive transfers to other hospitals, and cost cutting to the detriment of the quality of care.[21] They work under contract to the Health Care Financing Administration, the agency of the Department of Health and Human Services that administers medicare.[22] Most of them are responsible for a single state, but some cover two states, and one covers three. As stipulated by the 1982 legislation, their contracts set forth the so-called scope of work, specific tasks and goals for the contract period, as well as the budget they will receive. The first set of contracts, signed in 1984, and the second, signed in 1986, were each for two years. The third set of contracts will last three years and will be negotiated in batches—the first ones took effect October 1, 1988, the last ones April 1, 1990; some of the existing contracts will be extended in order to introduce this staggered schedule. The Health Care Financing Administration also contracts with an organization, called the SuperPRO, whose function is to monitor the PROs, to be the watchdog of the watchdogs.

The basic tasks assigned to PROs have remained much the same since 1984, but the emphasis and the details—such as the procedures or percentages of cases subject to review—have changed as all the parties involved have gained experience with prospective payment. The PROs must review hospital admissions to determine whether they are necessary; check the accuracy of the diagnosis and procedure codes submitted by hospitals (since these determine the payment the hospital will receive); review outlier cases, which qualify for extra payments because of long stays or high costs; review readmissions and transfers to other hospitals; and approve certain procedures before admission. Each PRO sets specific, numerical objectives appropriate to its state; for example, in the first contract period, the Missouri PRO undertook to reduce hospital admissions by 10 percent, the Florida PRO to reduce admissions for lens procedures by 76 percent.[23]

To carry out these and other tasks involves the PROs in the time-consuming job of sampling and reviewing medical records, their primary day-to-day activity. More than 40 percent of all medicare admissions were reviewed during the first contract period; thanks to changes made in the contract requirements, only about 25 percent were reviewed during the second period.[24] Medical records reviewers, who are usually nurses, are the backbone of the PROs' staffs. Physicians, who review cases once possible problems have been identified, serve as consultants and also on the board of directors. Most PROs are sponsored by the state medical society, and all can call on a large number of physicians to act as reviewers.

During the first two years the PROs, at the direction of the Health Care Financing Administration, spent most of their time checking for abuses of the payment system that would lead to overpayments—unnecessary admissions, readmissions, transfers, and coding of cases in ways that led to higher DRG payments than justified.[25] Several government agencies and private experts studied the work of the PROs during this period and recommended that quality review be strengthened.[26] In the budget legislation passed in 1985 and 1986, Congress directed that greater emphasis be put on quality and less on other kinds of review. The Health Care Financing Administration responded by developing a checklist for the PROs to use in screening cases for problems. This checklist, or set of "generic screens" as they are often called, was the first step toward a common methodology for all the PROs. After several months of experimentation at the beginning of the second contract period, the screens were routinely applied to all cases selected for review, regardless of the reason they were selected. PROs can supplement these screens with additional ones of their own choice.

The generic screens are important because they are the foundation of the PROs' efforts to identify problems with the quality of care. The screens highlight events during a hospital stay that might signal poor quality care.[27] The reviewer looks for unscheduled returns to the operating room, infections acquired or injuries sustained while in the hospital, or unexpected death. The screens specify the conditions that suggest one of these events. For example, an infection that follows an invasive procedure, or a temperature more than two degrees above normal more than 72 hours after the patient's admission to the hospital, are conditions that point to an infection acquired in the hospital, possibly as a result of inadequate care. The screens define an unexpected death as one during or after elective surgery, or following a return to intensive care within 24 hours of being transferred out, or under other unusual circumstances. The reviewer is directed to look for various kinds of trauma suffered in the hospital that may signal poor care—falls, drug reactions, reactions to anesthesia or blood transfusion, bedsores, or serious complications not related to the original reason for the hospital admission.

As a further check on the adequacy of care, the screens direct the reviewer to evaluate the patient's condition at the time of discharge from the hospital. If the patient's pulse, temperature, or blood pressure was seriously abnormal within 24 hours of discharge, the discharge may have been premature or the care inadequate; the screens define what constitutes seriously abnormal in each case. If the patient was still receiving intravenous fluids or drugs, or had a wound that was still bleeding, or if abnormal test results were not dealt with, quality problems may be indicated. The reviewer also checks on the adequacy of the discharge plan—the plan for follow-up care after the patient leaves the hospital. An appropriate plan may require nursing home care, help from a home health agency, or follow-up visits to the doctor or hospital.

If one or more of these signs turns up in the record, the reviewer follows up with the hospital or doctor to determine whether the problem can be traced to inadequate care or is explained by other circumstances. When the quality of care appears to be the problem, the case is usually referred to a physician for further review.* If the physician confirms a quality problem, or a series of them, the courses of corrective action available are the same as for such problems as unnecessary admissions.[28] The PRO can review more of the provider's cases ("intensified review"), or it can change the timing of review, requiring approval before an admission rather than waiting until afterwards to review it. It can require the doctor to take a course or retain a consultant for the kinds of cases that have proved to be problems. The PRO can also deny payment for the care in question; it is now required to do so for inappropriate or unnecessary care, and for fraudulent claims. If the problems are serious or frequent, the PRO can recommend a sanction, either a fine or suspension from the medicare program for a time, which must be approved by the inspector general of the Department of Health and Human Services before it goes into effect.[29]

How well do these screens work? The question cannot be answered at this point. The screens were given to the PROs by the Health Care Financing Administration without any pilot testing beforehand, and there is no generally agreed standard against which to measure them. Common sense suggests they are a reasonable first step. Discussions

---

* The initial reviewer may use his or her judgment in deciding whether to refer a case involving problems with the discharge plan, a fall, or a hospital-acquired infection, although the record must show that a problem was found even if nothing further was done.

with staff of the PROs show that they find them helpful simply because they encourage attention to quality and because they are used by all PROs.[30]

How many quality problems do the PROs discover, and how does this figure compare with the numbers of problems found by other groups? To answer these questions, the inspector general of Health and Human Services turned again to the sample of more than 7,000 medicare patients admitted between October 1984 and March 1985, well into prospective payment but before the generic screens were in use.[31] Defining poor quality as "medical care *clearly* failing to meet professionally recognized standards under any circumstances in any locale," the study found that 6.6 percent of the patients received poor care, most often because essential services were omitted.* During the same period, PROs reported that only 0.8 percent of the cases they reviewed received poor care, and the SuperPRO reported a 3.0 percent rate. Both rates increased with the introduction of the generic screens, to 3.6 percent for the PROs and 9.1 percent for the SuperPRO. The inspector general found that hospitals with the highest rates of poor quality also had unusual numbers of unnecessary admissions and premature discharges. Small, rural, and nonteaching hospitals were more likely than others to have quality problems.

In early 1989 the PROs were directed to pay especially close attention to hospitals whose medicare death rates are higher than expected.[32] The Health Care Financing Administration has published these death rates annually since 1986 for hospitals that participate in the program.[33] Any death of a medicare patient within 30 days of admission to the hospital is counted, and deaths as a percentage of the hospital's medicare patients during the year are reported in total and for certain diagnostic groups.[34] Statistical techniques are used to project the expected mortality range for each hospital based on the characteristics of its patients.[35] A study undertaken by HCFA indicates that

---

* An equal number of hospitals in each of three size categories (less than 100 beds, 100–299 beds, and 300 or more beds) was selected for the study. When the sample patients were weighted to reflect the population of all medicare patients in all hospitals, the proportion receiving poor-quality care was 5.5 percent. See Health Data Institute, *National DRG Validation Study,* report prepared for the Office of Inspector General, Department of Health and Human Services (Lexington, Mass., November 1987), pp. v, vi; and Office of Inspector General, Office of Analysis and Inspections, *National DRG Validation Study: Quality of Patient Care in Hospitals,* OAI-09-88-00870 (Washington: Department of Health and Human Services, July 1989), p. 1.

hospitals with excessive death rates also tend to fail the quality screens more often than other hospitals.[36]

The PROs' authority has been extended by recent legislation to include other providers of medical care in addition to hospitals. Over a period of several years, they will begin to review the care delivered to medicare beneficiaries by health maintenance organizations, nursing homes, home health agencies, hospital outpatient departments, outpatient surgery centers, and physicians' offices.[37] The first step of the extension began with the second round of contracts, when review of care delivered by health maintenance organizations was included in the PROs' responsibilities. As part of the third round of contracts, surgery performed in hospital outpatient departments and in freestanding surgery centers will be reviewed for both quality and necessity. These contracts also include the first step toward reviewing the entire gamut of care: cases of readmission, now defined to include readmissions within 31 days of discharge, will be reviewed not only for the quality of the hospital care, but also for the quality of the "intervening care" provided between admissions. The review of care at these other sites may prove difficult: unlike inpatient hospital care, there are no common methods of record-keeping. Besides, ways of evaluating quality are less well developed and the resistance to review is greater.[38]

As the PRO system matures, Congress, the Department of Health and Human Services, and the public will want to assess its costs and benefits. How well are the PROs performing their many jobs, and what are the benefits to the nation? The benefits are potentially large. The PROs can, if they succeed, help ensure that the money medicare spends buys the best possible care for the elderly. In addition, they can help people make better decisions about their care by providing information about hospitals to the public, information such as mortality rates for some kinds of surgery and the number of patients who develop postoperative complications, as they are now required to provide on request.[39]

At the same time the PROs involve costs. Besides their own expenses, and the expenses incurred by doctors and hospitals and others dealing with them, the use of review and sanctions causes ill will.[40] Some have argued that the approach is inherently too punitive, and that it should be possible to develop a more cooperative process for improving quality.[41] Further, the PROs work for the Health Care Financing Administration and must respond to the priorities of that agency, which may prevent them from fulfilling their potential for the nation at large. How these costs weigh against the potential benefits, and whether similar benefits can be achieved by other means, remain to be seen.

Quality over the Longer Term

The issue of quality over the longer term comes back to the fundamental questions about prospective payment: what are we gaining, and what are we giving up? Over the longer term, the potential gain from prospective payment is lower costs for the medicare program (see chapter 5). The potential loss is some of the good health that could be purchased with a larger expenditure. So far, although the evidence is sketchy and there are some worrisome signs to be investigated, the loss of good health does not appear to be large. For a while at least, as hospitals become more efficient, it may be possible to realize substantial savings without settling for lower quality care.

Over the longer term, the loss may become more noticeable as the incentives of prospective payment, and the limits placed on hospital resources, have more time to play themselves out. Some of the incentives should improve quality if there is room for improvement; the fixed payment encourages hospitals to eliminate unnecessary services; to specialize in the kinds of care they do best, which is good for quality as well as efficiency; and to reduce complications, such as hospital-acquired infections, that cost the hospital more than they bring in revenues.[42] But others will clearly worsen quality. If payment rates are too low, hospitals will have to slow the adoption of beneficial new technologies, or cut the level of beneficial services. And the limits on payment for inpatient care could encourage hospitals to provide too little inpatient care and lean too heavily on substitutes. Further, as one observer has noted, "Because Medicare is such a large payer, its level of payment over time is likely to determine the nature of hospital services for all patients, not just Medicare patients."[43]

How much quality would the nation be willing to give up for greater savings? Perhaps none. The annual impact report for 1985, prepared for Congress by the Health Care Financing Administration, asserts that the goal of prospective payment is to "maximize the health status of the population at the lowest cost."[44] In testimony before Congress, the Congressional Budget Office stated, "The main objectives of the PPS are to lower the growth rate of Medicare's payments to hospitals and encourage efficiency in the provision of hospital care, while not adversely affecting its quality."[45] Neither of these statements contemplates trading any quality for further reductions in cost.

Others appear more willing to accept the possibility that some health may have to be traded for additional savings. Consider this statement by a former head of the Health Care Financing Administration: "Our goal is to assure that any given patient receives the maximum benefit in improved health for any given level of health care expenditure."[46] The goal here is the most health that can be purchased for a given amount of money but, depending on the amount of money, that may fall short of maximum health. Similarly, in its annual report for 1988, the Physician Payment Review Commission states that an effective strategy for controlling medicare's costs means that medicare "beneficiaries and their physicians must be willing to forego services of little or no benefit."[47] Such decisions will not be easy to make. Everyone can agree that services of no benefit should go. But not everyone will agree to cut services of little benefit, or will agree on which services qualify as offering little benefit.

The choice about how much health to buy is complicated by a little-appreciated problem: surprisingly often, the information about what services produce what outcomes is not good enough to show what the trade-off is. It is not clear whether benefits are being lost or not. Experts have stressed this difficulty:

> For at least some important practices, the existing evidence is of such poor quality that it is virtually impossible to determine even what effect the practice has on patients, much less whether that effect is preferable to the outcomes that would have occurred with other options.[48]

> If we cannot know with certainty when additional expenditures will bring no further benefits, then we also cannot know with certainty when cost controls will begin to threaten patient well-being or harm quality of care.[49]

To a considerable extent, the debate over cost versus quality is taking place in a vacuum. Nobody knows what the trade-off really is. In this context, the new focus on quality brought by prospective payment is a clear gain. Quality has always been important, but it is only now getting the concentrated attention it deserves. The incentives of prospective payment, and increasingly the regulatory and review machinery that go with it, can help generate better information about the choices between quality and cost. Decisions that must be made largely in ignorance now are likely to be better informed in the future.

CHAPTER FIVE

The Financial Impact of Prospective Payment

THE OVERRIDING purpose of prospective payment was to slow the growth of medicare's expenditures—the spectre of imminent bankruptcy lay behind its speedy passage by Congress. Thus a crucial test of the system's success is, Has it brought expenditures under control? The changes and dislocations in the medical care of the elderly since 1983 will be judged worthwhile in large part by whether they have produced substantial savings.

The evidence shows that medicare's expenditures have been successfully controlled. Actual expenditures for recent years and the most recent projections for future years are well below the levels projected before prospective payment. In 1980 dollars, expenditures by medicare's Hospital Insurance Trust Fund, which pays hospital bills, are now projected to be about $12 billion less in 1990 than was forecast even as recently as 1984. At the price level expected in 1990, this amounts to a saving of $18 billion in that year alone. The trust fund is expected to be able to cover its costs until shortly after the year 2000. All signs indicate that the medicare savings are genuine and not the result of shifting costs to other parties.

This chapter traces the recent history of the projections made for the Hospital Insurance Trust Fund. To check the possibility that the savings are partly offset by higher costs to others, the chapter also reports on trends in payments by medicare's Supplementary Medical Insurance Trust Fund, which covers doctors' services and outpatient care, on the expenses medicare beneficiaries pay out of their own pockets, and on expenditures by the rest of the medical care system. Finally, it reports on the financial condition of hospitals—their profitability— since the introduction of prospective payment.

The Hospital Insurance Trust Fund*

Bills for the services covered under Part A of medicare—principally hospital care, but also some skilled nursing home and home health care—are paid out of the Hospital Insurance Trust Fund, which is financed by an earmarked tax on wages.[1] Every year the fund's trustees publish a report projecting expenditures and revenues for the next 75 years and evaluating the soundness of the fund. The projections from the reports of the last decade provide a basis for estimating prospective payment's effects on medicare's expenditures.

Ten successive reports, published in the years 1979 through 1988, were used for the estimates presented here.[2] The trustees forecast expenditures based on assumptions about the future course of the economy, the use of medical services, and the life expectancy of medicare enrollees; the assumptions are published in each report. Thus the projections can vary from year to year because of changes in these assumptions, and also because of congressionally mandated changes in policy. Since the estimates are politically sensitive, they may be subject to manipulation for political purposes as well. Ten reports make it possible to judge whether the projections are consistent enough despite these sources of variation and bias to serve as a reasonable basis for estimating the effects of prospective payment on medicare's expenditures.

To show the trends accurately, the projections must be adjusted for the widely different inflation rates assumed in different reports. In the last decade the assumptions about inflation have changed dramatically. Because of the high inflation rates of the late 1970s and early 1980s, projections made at the beginning of the decade assumed that inflation would continue to be high, especially in the short term. As inflation wound down, successive reports made correspondingly lower assumptions about future price levels. The expenditures projected for any particular year would have declined over the decade for this reason alone, hence the importance of correcting for inflation in order to see the true effect of prospective payment. The adjustments use the trustees' assumptions about inflation, which are published in full in the

* The estimates presented in this section were first published by Louise B. Russell and Carrie Lynn Manning in "The Effect of Prospective Payment on Medicare Expenditures," *New England Journal of Medicine*, vol. 320 (February 16, 1989), pp. 439–44. Tables 5-1 to 5-3 are reprinted with permission.

TABLE 5-1. Projected Expenditures of Medicare's Hospital Insurance Trust Fund Adjusted for Inflation, 1980–2000[a]

Billions of 1980 dollars

Year of Trustees' Report	1980	1985	1990	1995	2000
1979	24.80	38.15	55.87	[b]	[b]
1980	24.80	34.33	50.94	[b]	[b]
1981	25.60	35.65	55.19	[b]	[b]
1982	25.60	38.56	[b]	[b]	[b]
1983	25.60	39.79	54.20	[b]	[b]
1984	25.60	39.88	54.33	[b]	[b]
1985	25.60	37.78	46.62	60.38[c]	76.56[c]
1986	25.60	37.55	47.49	62.68	[b]
1987	25.60	37.55	44.92	57.69	70.09
1988	25.60	37.55	42.71	55.30	68.37

SOURCE: Louise B. Russell and Carrie Lynn Manning, "The Effect of Prospective Payment on Medicare Expenditures," *New England Journal of Medicine*, vol. 320 (February 16, 1989), p. 441. Reprinted with permission.

a. Series II projections. Starting in 1981, when two variants of series II were presented, the numbers shown are the average of II-A and II-B. The italicized numbers are actual expenditures in that year. Expenditures are adjusted for inflation using the price levels assumed in the report.

b. Trust fund depleted. For years in which the projections indicate that the trust fund would be depleted, the expenditures are not published.

c. Projection II-A only; projection II-B resulted in the trust fund being depleted in 2000.

same year's annual report of the trustees of the Old Age, Survivors, and Disability Insurance (Social Security) Trust Fund.

After adjustment for inflation, the projections made in the years before prospective payment turn out to be remarkably similar to one another (table 5-1). Consider the year 1990. In the reports for 1979 through 1984 the trustees consistently projected expenditures for 1990 of $54 billion to $56 billion in 1980 dollars. While the last year, 1984, was a prospective payment year, it was too soon to show the effects of the new system, and the projections reflect that. Thus the average projection of 1990's expenditures, in 1980 dollars, was about $55 billion just before prospective payment.

The sole exception is the considerably lower estimate made in the 1980 report. The reason for the low estimate in this year was an unusual assumption about the quantity of resources used in the course of a hospital admission. After decades of steady growth, the rate of increase in resources per admission slowed sharply in 1979. The trustees assumed that resources per admission would actually *decline* in 1980 and would stay below the long-term trend until 1982.[3] Subsequent events did not support their assumption, and the rates of increase for

1980 and later years (and even for 1979) were raised again in the next year's report. That the exception occurred in an election year suggests that the estimates may occasionally be manipulated, but the consistency of the remaining estimates indicates that it does not happen often.

In 1985, partway through the second year of prospective payment, the trustees lowered their estimate for 1990 to $47 billion in inflation-adjusted dollars. The next year's report published a similar estimate. In the reports of 1987 and 1988 the projection for 1990 dropped still further—to $43 billion in the later year. The difference between projections made at the beginning and the end of the decade was thus about $12 billion. Translated into the price level now expected in 1990, that means expenditures will be roughly $18 billion less in that year than they were expected to be before prospective payment.

Part of the saving came from an unexpected source—the decline in admissions that occurred with prospective payment. If admissions had remained at the level of 1980, future expenditures would be higher than currently projected, even with the restraining effect of the prospective rates. Table 5-2 shows the projections of each year three ways: in current dollars, that is, in the price level expected for that year at the time the projections were made; in 1980 dollars; and in 1980 dollars adjusted for the assumed changes in the admission rate. Because it is adjusted for changes in the admission rate, this last number shows what expenditures would be if both admissions and the price level had remained at the levels of 1980. Comparing this number with expenditures adjusted only for inflation shows the contribution of lower admissions to savings.

Starting with the 1986 report, by which time the decline in admissions was clearly established, projected expenditures adjusted for admissions and inflation are higher than those adjusted for inflation alone. In that report, $2.6 billion of the saving for 1990 was due to lower admissions ($50.13 billion − $47.49 billion). By the 1988 report, more than $4 billion of the saving was due to lower admissions. Thus about a third of the saving projected for 1990 comes, not from the prospective rates themselves, but from the accompanying decline in admissions.

Some of the saving in Part A may be offset by higher expenditures under Part B of medicare. The use of some services paid for by Part B, such as outpatient surgery, has increased because of prospective payment, and accounts in the press report that Part B expenditures are growing faster than expected.[4] The trustees of the Supplementary

TABLE 5-2. Projected Expenditures of Medicare's Hospital
Insurance Trust Fund, in Current Dollars, Adjusted for Inflation,
and Adjusted for Inflation and Changes in the Admission Rate,
1980–2000[a]

Billions of dollars

Year of Trustees' Report	1980	1985	1990	1995	2000
1979					
Current dollars	24.80	48.50	86.40	[b]	[b]
1980 dollars	24.80	38.15	55.87	[b]	[b]
1980 dollars adjusted for admissions	24.80	37.22	53.41	[b]	[b]
1980					
Current dollars	24.80	52.00	105.70	[b]	[b]
1980 dollars	24.80	34.33	50.94	[b]	[b]
1980 dollars adjusted for admissions	24.80	33.15	48.22	[b]	[b]
1981					
Current dollars	25.60	52.55	96.65	[b]	[b]
1980 dollars	25.60	35.65	55.19	[b]	[b]
1980 dollars adjusted for admissions	25.60	34.43	52.25	[b]	[b]
1982					
Current dollars	25.60	54.45	[b]	[b]	[b]
1980 dollars	25.60	38.56	[b]	[b]	[b]
1980 dollars adjusted for admissions	25.60	36.87	[b]	[b]	[b]
1983					
Current dollars	25.60	52.05	85.05	[b]	[b]
1980 dollars	25.60	39.79	54.20	[b]	[b]
1980 dollars adjusted for admissions	25.60	36.54	47.08	[b]	[b]
1984					
Current dollars	25.60	52.65	88.60	[b]	[b]
1980 dollars	25.60	39.88	54.33	[b]	[b]
1980 dollars adjusted for admissions	25.60	35.85	45.10	[b]	[b]
1985					
Current dollars	25.60	48.80	74.30	114.35[c]	160.10[c]
1980 dollars	25.60	37.78	46.62	60.38	76.56
1980 dollars adjusted for admissions	25.60	36.99	42.67	51.82	62.51
1986					
Current dollars	25.60	48.40	73.85	115.85	[b]
1980 dollars	25.60	37.55	47.49	62.68	[b]
1980 dollars adjusted for admissions	25.60	40.04	50.13	62.02	[b]
1987					
Current dollars	25.60	48.40	68.10	104.05	150.20
1980 dollars	25.60	37.55	44.92	57.69	70.09
1980 dollars adjusted for admissions	25.60	40.65	48.08	57.89	66.92
1988					
Current dollars	25.60	48.40	65.10	100.30	147.35
1980 dollars	25.60	37.55	42.71	55.29	68.37
1980 dollars adjusted for admissions	25.60	40.65	47.10	57.17	67.60

SOURCE: Same as table 5-1.
 a. Series II projections. Starting in 1981, when two variants of series II were presented, the numbers shown
are the average of II-A and II-B. The italicized numbers are actual expenditures in that year. Expenditures are
adjusted using the price levels and the growth in the admissions rate assumed in the report.
 b. See table 5-1, note b.
 c. See table 5-1, note c.

TABLE 5-3. Expenditures of Medicare's Supplementary Medical Insurance Trust Fund, in Current Dollars and Adjusted for Inflation, 1978–90[a]

Billions of dollars

Year	Current dollars	1980 dollars	Percent change in 1980 dollars
1978	7.80	9.69	...
1979	9.30	10.57	9.1
1980	11.20	11.20	6.0
1981	14.00	12.73	13.7
1982	16.20	13.85	8.8
1983	19.00	15.82	14.2
1984	20.60	16.48	4.2
1985	23.90	18.53	12.4
1986	27.30	20.84	12.5
1987	31.70	23.31	11.9
1988	36.10	25.60	9.8
1989	40.70	27.79	8.6
1990	46.30	30.33	9.1

SOURCE: Russell and Manning, "Effect of Prospective Payment," p. 442.
   a. The numbers shown are the average of series II-A and II-B. Expenditures are adjusted for inflation using the price levels given in Trustees of the Federal Supplementary Medical Insurance Trust Fund, *1988 Annual Report of the Board of Trustees*, H. Rept. 100-194, 100 Cong. 2 sess. (Government Printing Office, 1988), table 6. Figures for 1988, 1989, and 1990 are projections.

Medical Insurance Trust Fund, which pays Part B bills, have also expressed concern about rapidly rising costs, noting that expenditures have doubled in the last five years.[5] The problem did not begin with prospective payment, however—the 1987 report pointed out that expenditures had doubled every five or six years over a longer period.[6]

Expenditures for Part B, again adjusted for inflation, may have grown somewhat faster in recent years (table 5-3).[7] If the unusually high growth in real expenditures between 1982 and 1983 is omitted, as possibly reflecting anticipation of prospective payment, the average growth rate was 9.4 percent before prospective payment (1979–82) and 10.3 percent for 1984–87, the prospective payment years for which experience was complete at the time of the trustees' 1988 report. If the 1982–83 spurt is included, the rates are virtually identical for the two periods—10.4 percent versus 10.3 percent. The rates for the remaining years, 1987–90, show that the trustees expect the real growth in Part B expenditures to slow down.

Even if the rate for 1982–83 is omitted, the effect of the higher average under prospective payment is not large. Applying the average

growth rate for 1979–82 to the expenditures for 1983 and projecting
to 1990 yields an estimate of $29.7 billion, only $0.6 billion less than
the estimate that incorporates the growth rates actually experienced.
Thus when the saving to the Hospital Insurance Trust Fund and the
additional cost to the Supplementary Medical Insurance Trust Fund
are combined, the net saving to medicare in 1990 is still more than $11
billion in 1980 dollars, and about $17 billion in 1990 dollars.

Prospective payment has contributed substantially to the health of
the Hospital Insurance Trust Fund and the medicare program. In their
1988 report the trustees projected that the trust fund would not run
out of money until at least 2005 under their "intermediate" projections, those based on the assumptions they believe are most likely to
turn out to be correct. Although this is a considerable improvement
over the prospects of only a few years ago, they warned that the situation did not warrant complacency. "Because of the . . . probability that
the HI trust fund will be exhausted shortly after the end of this century,
the Board believes that early corrective action is essential in order to
avoid the need for later, potentially precipitous changes. The Board,
therefore, urges that the Congress take early remedial measures to
bring future HI program costs and financing into balance, and to
maintain an adequate trust fund against contingencies." [8]

Enrollees' Out-of-Pocket Expenses

Medicare coverage is subject to a number of deductibles and copayments.[9] Enrollees must pay a deductible ($560 in 1989) if they are
admitted to the hospital, and until 1989 they were liable for copayments if their stays lasted more than 60 days or if they used more than
20 days of skilled-nursing facility care after leaving the hospital. They
must pay the first $75 dollars of physicians' bills ($60 before 1982)
and 20 percent of reasonable charges after that point. If the doctor's
bill exceeds the medicare-determined "reasonable charge," the enrollee is responsible for the difference. In addition, enrollees pay a premium for coverage under Part B—$335 a year in 1989.[10]

Because of the way these enrollee payments are structured, hospital
stays are usually more completely covered by medicare than are other
services. The shift away from inpatient hospital care and toward nursing home, home health, and outpatient care has raised concern that
the elderly may be paying more out of their own pockets than before

TABLE 5-4. Enrollees' Out-of-Pocket Expenses for Services Covered by Medicare, 1980–87[a]

Year	Billions of dollars	As a percent of total medicare expenditures	Dollars per enrollee
1980	9.9	22.8	348
1981	11.6	22.3	400
1982	14.2	23.0	481
1983	16.2	23.1	540
1984	18.1	23.3	594
1985	18.8	22.5	605
1986	20.4	22.4	643
1987	22.6	22.9	697

SOURCES: Prospective Payment Assessment Commission, *Medicare Prospective Payment and the American Health Care System: Report to the Congress* (Washington, June 1988), p. 78, tables 4-1, 4-2. Amounts per enrollee were calculated using total medicare enrollment for all areas, in Part A and/or Part B, from the U.S. Bureau of the Census, *Statistical Abstract of the United States, 1987* (U.S. Department of Commerce, 1986), p. 356, table 604, for 1980–85 and the Health Care Financing Administration, Bureau of Data Management and Strategy, for 1986 and 1987.

a. Out-of-pocket expenses include deductibles, coinsurance, physician charges over and above the "reasonable charge" paid by medicare, and premiums for Part B coverage, all of which are paid by the enrollee. Medicaid pays deductibles, coinsurance, and premiums for some of the poor elderly.

prospective payment. This concern has been given visible shape by recent, large increases in the hospital deductible and the Part B premium, both of which are adjusted every year. The hospital deductible, for example, rose from $400 in 1985 to $492 in 1986, primarily because the cost per hospital day on which it was based rose sharply when lengths of stay dropped after the introduction of prospective payment.

Congress has responded to these concerns by limiting some increases in the amounts enrollees must pay.[11] Legislation that took effect in 1984 froze doctors' fees and included incentives for them to "accept assignment," which means that they also agree to accept the medicare-determined reasonable charge as payment in full; the number of doctors accepting assignment rose rapidly in the next few years. The Part B premium for 1986 was held at the level of 1985 (although two large increases then followed). In 1986, Congress set the increases in the hospital deductible for the next two years below the amounts called for by the usual formula and stipulated that future increases would be tied to the rise in prospective payment rates.

Out-of-pocket expenses have risen substantially in recent years but, partly because of the restraints introduced by Congress, they have not increased as a share of all spending on services covered by medicare (table 5-4). Payments per enrollee rose from $348 in 1980 to $697 in 1987, considerably faster than the rate of inflation. Yet as a percentage of the combined spending by the program and enrollees together on services covered by medicare, out-of-pocket expenses held steady at about 23 percent throughout the period. There are no data to show whether the shift in patterns of care means that extremely high out-of-pocket expenses are more of a problem than before prospective payment. While all enrollees pay the Part B premium, only those who use services pay the deductibles and coinsurance amounts, and some of their payments may be far higher than the averages suggest.

Thus, while out-of-pocket expenses have risen, they have not risen faster than total spending on medicare services, nor are enrollees paying a larger share than in the past. The catastrophic insurance program approved by Congress in June of 1988 will, by placing upper limits on the amounts enrollees must pay, help keep them from rising too rapidly in the future.[12] The first phase of the catastrophic program began January 1, 1989, by limiting enrollees' payments for hospital care to one hospital deductible a year and expanding coverage of nursing home care.[13] Coverage will be added for high physicians' bills in 1990 and for an expense medicare has never covered, outpatient prescription drugs, in 1991. While out-of-pocket expenses continue to be a problem for many of the elderly, it does not appear that prospective payment has made the problem worse, and the new catastrophic insurance program should make it better.

Other Payers

Since the passage of prospective payment, there has been considerable concern that, by reducing its own expenditures, medicare would simply shift costs to other payers, particularly private health insurers, because hospitals would make up their losses by charging these payers more. Thus the savings to medicare might be offset by higher expenditures elsewhere.

Several recent studies conclude that cost shifting has not occurred. If anything, the effects of prospective payment have spilled out beyond the medicare population and helped to reduce costs for other groups as well. These studies examine the effects of prospective payment on the Blue Cross and Blue Shield plans (which insure a larger share of the U.S. population than any other private insurer), on total hospital revenues, and on total national expenditures for all medical care.

Using quarterly data for the 62 Blue Cross plans for the years 1980–86, Scheffler and his colleagues looked at how prospective payment had affected inpatient and outpatient hospital use by, and the hospital expenses of, Blue Cross enrollees.[14] They concluded that prospective payment saved Blue Cross money; the savings appear to be due to a decline in admissions beyond what could have been expected from existing trends and the plans' own cost-containment efforts. In an examination of total hospital revenues—a measure that reflects use by medicare as well as other patients—Sloan and his colleagues found that revenue per capita was significantly reduced by prospective payment, indicating that savings by medicare were not matched by higher costs for other patients;[15] here again, fewer admissions appeared to be the reason. The Prospective Payment Assessment Commission has recently reported that prospective payment seems to have contributed to a slightly lower rate of growth in all medical expenditures in recent years.[16]

The agreement of these studies suggests that, if cost shifting has taken place, the amounts involved have not been large. Thus the savings to medicare appear to be genuine. Why prospective payment should be affecting other patients, when it was not intended to do so, has been a matter of some speculation. Both Scheffler and Sloan think that the answer may lie in "practice patterns," the habits physicians adopt when treating patients. If physicians and hospitals treat patients with similar medical conditions similarly, a major reform like prospective payment, which forces changes in the treatment of a large group of patients, may lead to the same sorts of changes for all patients.

Hospitals

On average, hospitals have done very well during the first few years of prospective payment.[17] Although most hospitals are legally nonprofit organizations, they can and do make profits, in the sense that they take in more in revenues than they pay out in costs. By any of several widely reported measures, their profits, which had climbed steadily since the early 1970s, jumped to a historical high in 1984 (figure 5-1). Profits have declined since that year but, as of 1987, remained above the levels of the 1970s.

Although all sources agree on the trends, the level of profits depends on the definition used by the particular source. The most global definition, used by the American Hospital Association, is the *total margin*—all revenues minus all expenses, expressed as a percent of all revenues.[18] This definition includes non-medicare patients as well as

FIGURE 5-1. Hospital Profits: Total and Patient Operating Margins, 1970–87[a]

Margin (percent)

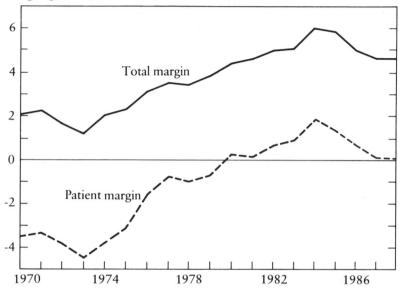

SOURCES: For 1980–87: Prospective Payment Assessment Commission, *Medicare Prospective Payment and the American Health Care System: Report to the Congress* (Washington, June 1988), p. 46. The margin for 1988 was estimated from data for the first eight months of the year from ProPAC, "PPS Costs, Revenue, and Margins: Preliminary Estimates, December 1988," Washington, December 14, 1988. Data are from the American Hospital Association National Hospital Panel Survey.
    a. See the text for definitions.

medicare patients, and income from endowment and other sources as well as payments for patient care; it subtracts all expenses from these revenues, whether or not they are related to patient care. By this definition, the peak reached in 1984 was a total margin of more than 6 percent, followed by a decline to approximately 5 percent by 1988 (figure 5-1).

The American Hospital Association also reports a second profit figure, which it calls the *patient margin,* to show how well payments received for taking care of patients cover the costs of that care.[19] This definition, like total margin, includes non-medicare as well as medicare patients, and outpatient as well as inpatient care. In keeping with the logic of the definition, the patient margin counts only revenues received as payment for taking care of patients. Less logically, it subtracts *total* costs from these revenues, not just the costs of patient care.[20] The difference is then expressed as a percent of patient revenues. Not surprisingly, the patient margin has always been less than the total margin and has often been negative. In 1973 it was between −4 percent and −5 percent (figure 5-1). At the 1984 peak it was positive and between 1 and 2 percent.

Because they include non-medicare patients, and outpatient as well as inpatient care, neither of these statistics shows how well prospective rates cover the costs of medicare admissions, or how vigorously hospitals have responded to them by cutting the costs of these admissions. The definition most commonly used for this purpose, sometimes called the *medicare operating margin* or the *PPS operating margin,* is based on medicare's inpatient payments and costs.[21] It is the difference between prospective payments received (including outlier payments) and operating costs incurred for medicare admissions, expressed as a percent of prospective payments. Costs are estimated from the medicare cost reports submitted by hospitals to the Health Care Financing Administration. The definition omits all items that are still paid on the basis of costs—capital, direct medical education, and bad debt; the profit margin on these items is zero by definition.

In 1984 and 1985, the first two years of prospective payment, the average medicare margin exceeded 14 percent.[22] In 1986 it declined to between 8 percent and 10 percent.[23] The numbers were so much higher than anyone had expected that they left the hospital industry defensive and the Congress open to suggestions that rates did not need to be raised much in the next few years.[24]

Part of the reason for the high profits, but only part, is that hospitals successfully controlled their costs. Between 1983 and 1984 costs per admission rose a little more than 1 percent.[25] A study of the first year of prospective payment shows that hospitals cut costs in direct proportion to the size of the threatened losses: hospitals that faced the largest potential shortfalls if they did nothing cut their costs the most, while those that foresaw little or no loss did the least.[26]

The profits also resulted, however, from unexpectedly high increases in revenues—payments per medicare case rose almost 16 percent between 1983 and 1984.[27] To begin, the rates for 1984 (and thus for later years as well) were set too high because they were based on unaudited cost data for 1981 that contained a number of errors; the inspector general estimated that the errors produced rates about 7 percent too high.[28] But payments were also higher than expected because of "DRG creep"—hospitals improved their reporting of cases to ensure that each case received the highest possible payment rate (see chapter 2). At the same time, as the simpler cases have been shifted to outpatient treatment, those still admitted to hospitals are more seriously ill. Thus the average DRG weight rose substantially following the introduction of prospective payment.

Although the annual update in the prospective rates has been held to very low levels (chapter 2), payments have continued to rise because of DRG creep. The Prospective Payment Assessment Commission estimates that policy decisions—that is, explicit decisions made about payment rates, such as the annual update—would have caused payments to increase 11 percent over the first five years of prospective payment.[29] The complexity of cases has increased so much, however, because of better coding and the shift of less seriously ill patients out of the hospital, that payments actually increased more than 31 percent over the period. This increase outpaced the 16 percent rise in the prices of goods and services hospitals use by a wide margin.

Since 1984 the cost per case for medicare patients has risen as fast or faster than prospective payments, and profit margins on medicare patients have begun to decline.[30] Observers have speculated that hospitals reacted with particular vigor in the first year to provide themselves with a margin of safety amid the uncertainties of the new payment system, and that their very success made it unnecessary to cut costs in subsequent years.[31] Profits on medicare admissions are estimated to have averaged between 4.5 and 6.3 percent in 1987 and close to zero in 1988.[32]

Not all hospitals have fared equally well, of course, and the inequities have played an important part in the changes legislated in payment rates since 1984.[33] The big winners have been large, urban hospitals, and particularly teaching hospitals—the medicare margin of teaching hospitals averaged almost 18 percent in 1984 and 11 percent in 1987.[34] Rural hospitals have not done nearly as well: their medicare margin in 1984 was just under 6 percent, but by the third and fourth years of prospective payment, most rural hospitals were losing money on medicare patients. The persistent disparity between urban and rural hospitals fueled the debate over the differences in their rates and led to several changes designed to reduce those differences, including a larger annual update for rural hospitals in 1988 and 1989 (see chapter 2).

The variation in profitability notwithstanding, the financial success of hospitals has been reassuring. Early concerns that hospitals might not be able to cope with the new system have turned out to be unwarranted: most have done well and gradual adjustments in the rate system are helping many of the rest.

The longer-term issue that remains is the appropriate level of profits. Although the opportunity to make profits was built into prospective payment to encourage hospitals to be more efficient, the high levels actually achieved have caused surprise and even shock. Congress responded with low rate increases after the first year. The hospital industry, with some sense of grievance, argues that this amounts to taking away the rewards that were promised for efficiency, and that, rather than being penalized with low increases, they should be allowed to keep their profits and to receive increases that at least match inflation.[35]

Some profit is essential. No matter how carefully the rates are set, in an imperfect world they will never match the costs of efficiently run hospitals exactly, and a margin of safety is necessary.[36] But what level of profits is reasonable, as an incentive and as a safety margin? This question comes back to the issue, discussed in chapter 2 and again in chapter 4, of the bases on which rates are set. How well is efficiency represented by the factors used to set the rates, and how well could it be represented by any available measures? What quality of care should the rates provide? The legitimacy of profits depends on the legitimacy of the rates, and if rates are not, or cannot be, set to reward efficiency and penalize inefficiency with reasonable accuracy, and if the quality of care that should be provided cannot be agreed upon, profits will continue to be a matter of controversy.

CHAPTER SIX

Conclusions

IN 1983 medicare replaced its cost-based method of reimbursing hospitals with a prospective payment system. Hospitals now face fixed rates, set in advance, for each admission and must keep the costs of care below the rates to avoid losses. From the start, the new system was recognized as revolutionary—one that might well bring medicare's spiraling expenditures under control, but that promised at the same time to change the medical sector in major ways. After six years of experience with prospective payment, a preliminary evaluation of the system's success is in order. The important questions are provided by the issues that dominated the congressional debate in 1983: How much has prospective payment saved? And what effects, good or bad, has it had on the care of the elderly?

A Preliminary Assessment

Prospective payment has changed the way care is given to elderly patients in the United States, causing a large shift away from inpatient hospital care and toward other kinds of care (chapter 3). Except for the fall in hospital admissions, the changes are logical consequences of the incentives created by prospective rates. Admissions of the elderly fell for several years after 1983, even though hospitals could have collected more revenue by increasing admissions, probably because of the monitoring system instituted by the Health Care Financing Administration exactly to prevent an increase. The average length of stay for medicare patients dropped by a full day between 1983 and 1984 as hospitals looked for ways to cut costs. The use of tests and procedures has also declined. Because of fewer admissions and shorter stays, hospitals are struggling to cope with the lowest occupancy rates in four decades.

Many more patients are now receiving part or all of their care outside the hospital (chapter 3). Sometimes the alternatives substitute for a hospital stay; sometimes they complete the care that started in the hospital and that, before prospective payment, might have been completed there. The number of patients referred to home health care after discharge from the hospital jumped sharply after 1983. Although the number discharged to nursing homes has not changed much, the percentage of deaths among those aged 65 or older that takes place in nursing homes has risen, while the percentage in hospitals has declined, indicating that nursing homes increasingly care for terminally ill patients. Many surgical procedures once performed during a hospital admission are now routinely performed on outpatients, either in hospital outpatient departments or freestanding surgery centers. Hospitals are expanding their outpatient departments and adding services such as home health care to take advantage of the rising demand for these alternatives and to offset the loss of inpatient business.

As dramatic as these changes are, their importance lies not in themselves but in their implications for costs and for the quality of care. Prospective payment has succeeded in its primary objective, slowing the growth of medicare spending (chapter 5). Expenditures from the Hospital Insurance Trust Fund, which pays hospital bills, are running substantially below the levels projected before prospective payment was passed: they are now expected to be $18 billion less in 1990 than was estimated in the early 1980s—a saving of about 20 percent. Even when extra spending for outpatient care, possibly due to prospective payment, is deducted, the net saving in 1990 is more than $17 billion. Studies of other payers show that the savings have not been achieved at their expense, as was initially feared might be the case. If anything, prospective payment has reduced their expenditures as well as those of the medicare program.

What the changes mean for the quality of care received by patients is less easy to determine (chapter 4). After dropping substantially during the 1970s, the death rate of the elderly has not shown any definite trend in the 1980s, before or after the introduction of prospective payment—it dipped in 1984, rose in 1985, and dipped back to the level of 1984 in 1986. Other, indirect measures of quality, such as readmissions to hospitals or transfers to other institutions, offer no clear-cut signals that prospective payment has brought ill effects. One study found that the number of elderly admitted to hospitals through emergency rooms has risen significantly under prospective payment, a possible sign of problems, but further investigation will be required to decide what this means.[1]

Indeed, a major obstacle to evaluating what has happened to the quality of care is the scarcity of information about it (chapter 4). Before prospective payment, no system existed to evaluate quality on a national or regional scale. Mechanisms and data have been rapidly assembled, but too late to compare what is happening now with the situation before 1983. It is only slowly becoming possible to evaluate changes in quality from one year to the next as prospective payment continues, or differences from one place to the next. The lack of historical information on any but the crudest measures, such as the death rate, may mean that it will be impossible ever to find out whether and how quality has changed.

Studies based on patient records from the files of hospitals and other providers, although difficult and expensive to undertake, can overcome some of the problems and provide illuminating insights. Two studies of elderly patients with hip fractures, cited in chapter 4, found that, after the introduction of prospective payment, hospital stays were shorter and many more patients were discharged to nursing homes at the end of the hospital stay.[2] Those facts in themselves do not indicate a problem, but disturbingly, many more patients were *still* in nursing homes six months to a year after discharge. One of the studies suggested that the problem might not be an inevitable consequence of prospective payment. It found that patients enrolled in a health maintenance organization, apparently similar in all respects to those who were not, were more likely to be discharged to a nursing home, but less likely to be there at the end of a year. This finding suggests that there may be ways of caring for patients that successfully compensate for shorter hospital stays, ways that are not yet in general use.

Toward Better Quality Care

The new concern with quality, aroused by fears that hospitals may be too zealous in cutting costs under prospective payment, has the potential to bring major gains. Until 1983 quality was largely taken for granted on the assumption that, as long as money was freely available to pay for it, care of high quality would be forthcoming. This view overlooked other causes of poor quality, including the possibility that it could be a matter of doing too much as well as too little. In addition, the true state of quality was then, and remains, difficult to assess because of the large gaps in knowledge about what works—what services produce what outcomes for which patients. Now that quality is recognized as something that will not take care of itself, data systems and review mechanisms must be developed to monitor, measure, and encourage its existence (chapter 4).

The creation of the Peer Review Organizations (PROs) to review quality was a potentially important step in this direction (chapter 4). A basic requirement for their successful operation is that information be reported the same way by all providers. Under prospective payment, for the first time, all acute-care hospitals use the same diagnosis and procedure codes, and the same forms, to report cases for payment. The PROs started work with a charge from the Health Care Financing Administration (HCFA) that stressed checking for errors leading to overpayment—unnecessary admissions, incorrect codes, and the like. In 1986, in response to congressional insistence that more attention be paid to quality, the HCFA supplied the PROs with a set of "generic screens," essentially checklists, for evaluating the quality of care provided in all cases reviewed, whatever the reason for their initial selection. The introduction of a common methodology for quality review was another step toward better care.

The more difficult job of extending quality review to other settings—nursing homes, home health agencies, hospital outpatient departments, and physicians' offices—lies ahead. The quality of care in these settings is more important than ever because they are being used more frequently, to keep patients out of hospitals or shorten their stays. PROs are just beginning to review these providers—health maintenance organizations are already being reviewed, and outpatient surgery and the care provided between related hospital admissions will be added in the round of contracts signed during 1988–90. To review all care outside hospitals, the PROs will have to introduce new data systems and review methods. Record-keeping in many of these settings has never approached the completeness or uniformity that was true of hospitals even before prospective payment, nor have many of them been subject to review before.[3]

To provide a better basis for future quality review, the Health Care Financing Administration is combining its data files to allow researchers to study all the care received by a patient during an episode of illness, at least all the care paid for by medicare.[4] The HCFA also plans to make millions of medicare records more easily available to researchers, so that analyses can be done to find out "what works," that is, which treatments are effective and which are not.[5] This will help to address the problem of inadequate information about the effectiveness of different kinds of care. Still, the effort is limited by medicare's records: they include little in the way of direct measures of health outcomes, and they omit services not paid for by medicare, of which most nursing home care is an especially important example.

In future the effort to review and evaluate quality must try to focus on complete episodes of care. More and more patients are being cared for by several different providers during the course of an illness, and the important question is not how well each provider performs individually, but how well they work together; the ultimate measure of quality is not whether the patient leaves the hospital sooner, and perhaps sicker, than before, but how well the patient is when care is complete and how long it takes to reach that point. Again, the differences between HMO and other patients in the study of hip fractures point to the critical importance of evaluating care as a whole, not as separate components. To review the quality of care over an episode, analysts will need to link detailed information about the care delivered to the patient in different settings—what services were delivered by whom and when—and to link that record to the final health of the patient. No record-keeping systems are yet capable of doing this, and creating such systems should be a matter of high priority.

The evaluation of quality is too important to be left to the Health Care Financing Administration alone. It is essential that others get involved in studying quality in order to be sure that the picture is accurate in all important respects. Even small studies can raise questions that may not be raised by the agency directly responsible for administering medicare. More generally, other researchers may have access to information, or see problems and possibilities, that the HCFA and the PROs do not.

The evaluation of quality deserves a national effort involving many parties. That effort would be more effective if some institution with national standing as an impartial leader—perhaps the Institute of Medicine or a major foundation—supported the development of a research agenda to guide it. The agenda should spell out the issues that need to be addressed, set priorities among them, and suggest the best approaches for addressing them. With some such overall guidance, the efforts of individual researchers would be more likely to produce complete and important information about quality.

The Rate-Setting System

The basic elements of the rate-setting system originally approved by Congress are still in place after six years (chapter 2). Rates are set prospectively for the admission or "case," and adjusted for the hospital's location (urban or rural), the patient's diagnosis (DRG), the wage level of hospitals in the area, and the hospital's teaching activity. They are increased each year by an annual update factor decided by Congress. While many changes have been proposed, and some have been accepted—for example, the teaching adjustment has been reduced, and an adjustment for hospitals serving a disproportionate share of poor people added—the basic framework of the system is unchanged.

Even those who propose "major" reforms appear to accept the basic outline of the system. The American Hospital Association, for example, has called for the use of a single national standardized amount, with no distinction between urban and rural hospitals, which would be recalculated every four years on the basis of current cost information.[6] Besides operating costs, allowances for working capital and charity care would be included. To produce payment rates for individual cases, the standardized amount would be adjusted for prices in the local area (for nonlabor inputs as well as labor), and for the patient's diagnosis and the severity of his or her condition. Between recalculations, the rates would automatically be increased each year in line with inflation in the prices of goods and services hospitals buy. The association argues that this approach would give hospitals a more predictable flow of revenues and allow them to retain a reasonable level of profits, while reassuring the government that every four years it would be able to capture some of the savings by recalculating the rates on the basis of new cost information.

In another proposal, a group of researchers has recommended that rates be set individually for each hospital based on its own costs, not just as a transitional device but permanently.[7] Separate rates would be set for patients with different diagnoses, and, each year, the rates would be increased by the same percentage for all hospitals, in the manner of the annual update now. The authors of this proposal believe a system that distributes money according to historic costs, and thus much as it was distributed before prospective payment, is fairer than one that produces the major shifts of revenue among hospitals that have occurred under prospective payment (see chapter 5 on hospital profits). Their argument implies that fairness means similar profits, rather than the standard implicit in the current system—similar prices for specific products.

These proposals are, however, more remarkable for their agreement with the current system than for their differences. They do not challenge the idea that rates should be set prospectively or that they should be set for the hospital admission. They adjust rates using DRGs or something very like them. Both allow hospitals to keep any profits or to suffer the consequences of losses. Although many changes have been proposed, the need for a system much like the current one does not seem to be questioned.

Much of the debate over the current system has revolved around its fairness—the way it rewards some hospitals and not others. The issues include such questions as how labor markets should be defined, how the wage indexes should be calculated, whether DRGs can and should be further refined to reflect the severity of the patient's illness, the appropriate differentials, if any, between urban and rural hospitals, and so on (chapter 2). The Prospective Payment Assessment Commission has summed it up: "To ensure that PPS treats hospitals fairly, efforts to refine the technical base for payments must continue." [8]

In future, more attention should be focused on how prospective payment can encourage the best configuration of services for patients across the full range of care. The designers of prospective payment foresaw that it would lead to greater use of alternatives to hospital care. But their assignment was to control hospital costs, not to consider whether the incentives inherent in fixed rates for hospital admissions could or would lead to the best combinations of those alternatives, or would induce hospital care and the alternatives to develop in ways that best complement each other. With payment reforms now in the works for other kinds of care, notably physicians' services,* it is time to address that issue. It is unlikely that the elderly will be best served by separate and largely unrelated ways of paying for the services they need.

Again, the studies of hip fracture patients suggest that HMOs' ex-

---

*A commission, the Physician Payment Review Commission, has been created to recommend reforms to Congress. See Physician Payment Review Commission, *Annual Report to Congress, 1988* and *1989* (Washington, 1988, 1989).

perience may offer some useful guidance. They also point to the importance of nursing homes as part of many patients' care. Most nursing
home care is currently paid for by medicaid or by individuals, not by
medicare, and there are no financial links to encourage the coordina-
tion of hospital and nursing home care. Attention to these issues could
ultimately lead to a different type of payment system for hospitals as
well as other providers of medical care.

How Much for Medical Care?

The most important issue about prospective payment is not solely,
or even primarily, technical. It comes down to: how much does the
nation want to spend on the medical care of the elderly? And for what
standard of care? Since the elderly are such an important force in the
medical care system and their care sets standards for everyone, how
this issue is decided will have a lot to say about spending on everyone's
medical care.

The answers depend on the value the nation places on medical care
compared with other uses to which the national income could be put.
Resources devoted to medical care cannot be used for education, hous-
ing, roads, pensions, recreation, defense. The limits are especially obvious in an era when the federal government is running a deficit so
large that substantial cuts in public or private spending will be necessary simply to reduce it, let alone to increase spending for any purpose.

Not everyone agrees on how much should be spent (chapter 4). The
aim of prospective payment is often described as "to pay for necessary
care efficiently provided." The factors used to set rates are defended as
related to the costs of efficiently provided care, although their relation
to true efficiency, as opposed to costs incurred, is simply not known
(chapter 2). But many people recognize, or suspect, that all necessary
care, even efficiently provided, may be more care than the nation is
ready to pay for. If more savings are wanted, some beneficial services,
and thus some good health, will have to be sacrificed. How much to
give up, in return for how much in savings, is an issue that needs and
deserves regular debate. It also needs a more complete foundation of
information about the effectiveness of medical care: the choices are
obscured by the fact that the link between costs and health is so poorly
documented.

How high to set prospective rates is ultimately a decision about how
much to spend on medical care. The methods for setting prospective

rates provide the means for working out the balance between medical care and other priorities. The formula and cost information initially used to set rates determined the spending base and the distribution of spending. The annual updates determine the growth in spending, and when different updates are approved, allow changes in the distribution—as do alterations in the rate formula. Recalculation of the basic rates, which has not yet been done, would also allow spending to be adjusted to reflect changes in the consensus about how much should be spent.

Because the underlying issue is not technical, prospective payment does not and cannot work automatically. Nor would any alternative system. A rate-setting system is simply a mechanism for expressing how the nation values medical care for the elderly, and ultimately for everyone, compared with the things it must give up to provide that care. No system, prospective payment or cost reimbursement, will ever rest easily on an agreed-upon technical foundation. Instead, it sets ground rules for the annual debate during which the country decides how much to devote to medical care next year. So far prospective payment seems to be serving that purpose well.

NOTES

Chapter One

1. See Louise B. Russell, *Technology in Hospitals: Medical Advances and Their Diffusion* (Brookings, 1979).

2. Daniel R. Waldo, Katharine R. Levit, and Helen Lazenby, "National Health Expenditures, 1985," *Health Care Financing Review,* vol. 8 (Fall 1986), table 5; and Katharine R. Levit and others, "National Health Expenditures, 1984," *Health Care Financing Review,* vol. 7 (Fall 1985), table 8.

3. *1982 Annual Report of the Board of Trustees of the Federal Hospital Insurance Trust Fund,* H. Doc. 97-166, 97 Cong. 2 sess. (Government Printing Office, 1982).

4. Congressman W. Henson Moore in *Congressional Record,* March 9, 1983, p. 4507.

5. *Congressional Record,* July 19, 1982, pp. 16904–09; July 20, pp. 16978–80; and July 21, pp. 17195–212.

6. U.S. Department of Health and Human Services, "Report to Congress: Hospital Prospective Payment for Medicare," Washington, December 1982.

7. "Major Changes Made in Medicare Program," *Congressional Quarterly Almanac,* 98 Cong. 2 sess. (1983), vol. 39 (Washington, 1983), pp. 391–94; and Linda E. Demkovich, "Who Says Congress Can't Move Fast? Just Ask Hospitals about Medicare," *National Journal,* vol. 15 (April 2, 1983), pp. 704–07.

8. "Major Changes," *Congressional Quarterly Almanac,* p. 394.

9. *Congressional Record,* March 9, 1983, pp. 4511–12, 4549, 4564; March 16, pp. 5454–61, 5465–66; March 17, pp. 5897–900; March 18, pp. 6093–94, 6099–104; and March 22, p. 6605. Also Demkovich, "Who Says Congress Can't Move Fast?"

10. Sen. Charles E. Grassley made the point about the share of hospital costs; see *Congressional Record,* July 19, 1982, p. 16909.

11. *Congressional Record,* March 18, 1983, p. 6100. See also Sen. Edward M. Kennedy, March 18, 1983, pp. 6097–98; and Congressman Dan Rostenkowski, March 9, 1983, p. 4498; Congressman Moore, also March 9, p. 4507; and Congressman Andrew Jacobs, Jr., March 9, pp. 4511–12.

12. *Congressional Record,* March 17, 1983, p. 5897. See also *Congressional Record* for both the House and Senate for March 9, 16, 17, 18, and 22, as cited above, especially Congressman Jacobs, *Congressional Record,* March 9, 1983, p. 4512.

Chapter Two

1. Stuart Guterman and Allen Dobson, "Impact of the Medicare Prospective Payment System for Hospitals," *Health Care Financing Review,* vol. 7 (Spring 1986), pp. 97–114; Prospective Payment Assessment Commission (ProPAC), *Report and Recommendations to the Secretary, U.S. Department of Health and Human Services, 1985* (Washington, April 1, 1985), p. 17; and ProPAC, *Technical Appendixes to the Report and Recommendations to the Secretary, U.S. Department of Health and Human Services, 1985* (Washington, April 1, 1985), pp. 9–11.

2. 62 Fed. Reg. 33,034, 33,036 (1987).

3. Health Care Financing Administration, Office of Research and Demonstrations, *Report to Congress: Impact of the Medicare Hospital Prospective Payment System, 1985 Annual Report,* HCFA Pub. 03251 (Baltimore: U.S. Department of Health and Human Services, August 1987), p. 2.11; and information supplied by the HCFA.

4. Guterman and Dobson, "Impact of the Medicare Prospective Payment System," p. 101.

5. Guterman and Dobson, "Impact of the Medicare Prospective Payment System," p. 100; and ProPAC, *Technical Appendixes, 1985,* p. 4.

6. ProPAC, *1988 Adjustments to the Medicare Prospective Payment System: Report to the Congress* (Washington, November 1987), p. 19.

7. Congressional Budget Office, *Including Capital Expenses in the Prospective Payment System* (August 1988), p. 14.

8. ProPAC, *Technical Appendixes, 1985,* pp. 14–15, 23; and Louise B. Russell, "Medical Care," in Joseph A. Pechman, *Setting National Priorities: The 1984 Budget* (Brookings, 1983), pp. 131–33.

9. ProPAC, *Technical Appendixes, 1985,* pp. 3, 11–13, 17–19.

10. ProPAC, *1988 Adjustments,* p. 28; and Susan I. DesHarnais, James D. Chesney, and Steven T. Fleming, "Should DRG Assignment Be Based on Age?" *Medical Care,* vol. 26 (February 1988), pp. 124–31.

11. HCFA, Office of Research and Demonstrations, *Report to Congress— DRG Refinement: Outliers, Severity of Illness, and Intensity of Care,* HCFA Pub. 03254 (Baltimore: Department of Health and Human Services, September 1987), chap. 3.

12. ProPAC, *Technical Appendixes, 1985,* p. 81.

13. ProPAC, *Report and Recommendations to the Secretary, U.S. Department of Health and Human Services, 1986* (Washington, April 1, 1986), pp. 49–56.

14. ProPAC, *Technical Appendixes, 1985,* pp. 94–98; ProPAC, *1988 Ad-*

justments, pp. 22–23; and *Social Security Amendments of 1983*, H. Rept. 98-47, 98 Cong. 1 sess. (Government Printing Office, 1983), p. 187.

15. ProPAC, *Technical Appendixes, 1985*, pp. 11–13.

16. ProPAC, *1988 Adjustments*, p. 12; and ProPAC, *Report and Recommendations to the Secretary, U.S. Department of Health and Human Services, 1989* (Washington, March 1, 1989), pp. 65–67.

17. Guterman and Dobson, "Impact of the Medicare Prospective Payment System"; ProPAC, *Technical Appendixes, 1985*; and ProPAC, *1988 Adjustments*.

18. ProPAC, *Technical Appendixes, 1985*, p. 5.

19. ProPAC, *Technical Appendixes, 1985*, p. 66; and HCFA, *Report . . . DRG Refinement*, Pub. 03254, chap. 1.

20. 51 Fed. Reg. 31,463 (1986).

21. ProPAC, *Technical Appendixes, 1985*, pp. 5–6; *Social Security Amendments of 1983*, p. 189; and HCFA, *Report . . . DRG Refinement*, Pub. 03254, p. 7.

22. General Accounting Office, *Medicare: Indirect Medical Education Payments Are Too High*, GAO/HRD-89-33 (January 1989), p. 3.

23. 42 C.F.R. sec. 412.106 (1987).

24. Consolidated Omnibus Budget Reconciliation Act of 1985, P.L. 99-272; and Omnibus Budget Reconciliation Act of 1987, P.L. 100-203.

25. ProPAC, *1988 Adjustments*, p. 6; and ProPAC, *1989 Adjustments to the Medicare Prospective Payment System: Report to the Congress* (Washington, November 1988), p. 8.

26. ProPAC, *Technical Appendixes, 1985*, p. 27.

27. ProPAC, *Report and Recommendations to the Secretary, U.S. Department of Health and Human Services, 1987* (Washington, April 1, 1987), p. 26.

28. Guterman and Dobson, "Impact of the Medicare Prospective Payment System."

29. 47 Fed. Reg. 34,082 (1982) (legislated in Omnibus Budget Reconciliation Act of 1980, P.L. 96-499).

30. 52 Fed. Reg. 20,623 (1987); and 52 Fed. Reg. 20,466–67 (1987).

31. GAO, *Post-Hospital Care: Efforts to Evaluate Medicare Prospective Payment Effects Are Insufficient*, GAO/PEMD-86-10 (June 1986).

32. GAO, *Post-Hospital Care*; Russell, "Medical Care," p. 113; and Daniel R. Waldo, Katharine R. Levit, and Helen Lazenby, "National Health Expenditures, 1985," *Health Care Financing Review*, vol. 8 (Fall 1986), table 7.

33. Carrie Lynn Manning, "Peer Review Organizations," background paper prepared for this study, Brookings, 1988.

34. Allan M. Greenspan and others, "Incidence of Unwarranted Implantation of Permanent Cardiac Pacemakers in a Large Medical Population," *New England Journal of Medicine*, vol. 318 (January 21, 1988), pp. 158–63.

35. ProPAC, *1988 Adjustments*, p. 5.

36. Actual payments in that year, which were based on a blend of each

hospital's costs, a set of regional rates, and the national rates, matched 89 percent of the variation among hospitals. See HCFA, *Report . . . DRG Refinement,* Pub. 03254, summary and chap. 4, p. 4-31.

37. HCFA, *Report . . . DRG Refinement,* Pub. 03254, chap. 2.

38. HCFA, *Report . . . DRG Refinement,* Pub. 03254, esp. chap. 3.

39. HCFA, *Report . . . DRG Refinement,* Pub. 03254, p. 3-42.

40. "HCFA to Study High Cost Procedures," *McGraw-Hill's Medicine and Health,* vol. 42 (March 7, 1988), p. 2; and Richard Sorian, "1988: A Year in Review," *McGraw-Hill's Medicine and Health,* vol. 42 (December 26, 1988).

41. ProPAC, *Report and Recommendations, 1985; 1986; 1987;* and *1988.* Although ProPAC mentions the issue again in its 1989 report (p. 16), the report does not include a specific recommendation.

42. Jerry Cromwell and others, "Sources of Hospital Cost Variation by Urban-Rural Location," *Medical Care,* vol. 25 (September 1987), pp. 801–29.

43. ProPAC, *Report and Recommendations, 1987,* p. 45.

44. ProPAC, *Report and Recommendations, 1987,* p. 45.

45. "Rockefeller: Rural Hospitals Need Help," *McGraw-Hill's Medicine and Health,* vol. 42 (February 8, 1988).

46. ProPAC, *1988 Adjustments,* p. 10.

Chapter Three

1. Daniel R. Waldo, Katharine R. Levit, and Helen Lazenby, "National Health Expenditures, 1985," *Health Care Financing Review,* vol. 8 (Fall 1986), tables 5, 7.

2. U.S. Department of Health and Human Services, "Report to Congress: Hospital Prospective Payment for Medicare" (Washington, December 1982), p. 108.

3. "Are DRGs Effective?" *Washington Report on Medicine and Health,* vol. 38 (May 7, 1984); and "Monitoring of PPS Hospitals Increases," *Washington Report on Medicine and Health,* vol. 38 (October 22, 1984), p. 2.

4. Carrie Lynn Manning, "Peer Review Organizations," background paper prepared for this study, Brookings, 1988; "PRO Goals: Realistic or Risky?" *Washington Report on Medicine and Health,* vol. 38 (August 6, 1984); and Office of Inspector General, Office of Analysis and Inspections, *The Utilization and Quality Control Peer Review Organization (PRO) Program: Quality Review Activities,* OAI-01-88-00570 (Washington: Department of Health and Human Services, August 1988).

5. Prospective Payment Assessment Commission (ProPAC), *Technical Appendixes to the Report and Recommendations to the Secretary, U.S. Department of Health and Human Services, 1988* (Washington, March 1, 1988), pp. 113–15.

6. "Admissions Increase Will Cost Money," *Washington Report on Medicine and Health,* vol. 38 (January 30, 1984), p. 1.

7. Martin Ruther and Cheryl Black, "Medicare Use and Cost of Short-Stay Hospital Services by Enrollees with Cataract, 1984," *Health Care Financing Review,* vol. 9 (Winter 1987), pp. 91–99.

8. Susan DesHarnais, James Chesney, and Steven Fleming, "The Impact of the Prospective Payment System on Hospital Utilization and the Quality of Care: Trends and Regional Variations in the First Two Years," paper presented at the October 1987 meeting of the American Public Health Association, p. 9.

9. Susan DesHarnais and others, "The Early Effects of the Prospective Payment System on Inpatient Utilization and the Quality of Care," *Inquiry,* vol. 24 (Spring 1987), pp. 7–16; DesHarnais and others, "Impact of the Prospective Payment System"; and Health Care Financing Administration, Office of Research and Demonstrations, *Report to Congress: Impact of the Medicare Hospital Prospective Payment System, 1985 Annual Report,* HCFA Pub. 03251 (Baltimore: Department of Health and Human Services, August 1987), pp. 3.4–3.6.

10. Karen Beebe, Wayne Callahan, and Antonio Mariano, "Medicare Short-Stay Hospital Length of Stay, Fiscal Years 1981–85," *Health Care Financing Review,* vol. 7 (Spring 1986), pp. 119–25; and HCFA, *1985 Impact Report,* Pub. 03251, pp. 3.6–3.10.

11. David Barton Smith and Robert Pickard, "Evaluation of the Impact of Medicare and Medicaid Prospective Payment on Utilization of Philadelphia Area Hospitals," *Health Services Research,* vol. 21 (October 1986), pp. 529–46.

12. HCFA, *1985 Impact Report,* Pub. 03251; and DesHarnais and others, "Impact of the Prospective Payment System," p. 11.

13. HCFA, *1985 Impact Report,* Pub. 03251, pp. 6.10–6.14.

14. John F. Fitzgerald and others, "Changing Patterns of Hip Fracture Care before and after Implementation of the Prospective Payment System," *Journal of the American Medical Association,* vol. 258 (July 10, 1987), pp. 219–21.

15. John F. Fitzgerald, Patricia S. Moore, and Robert S. Dittus, "The Care of Elderly Patients with Hip Fracture: Changes since Implementation of the Prospective Payment System," *New England Journal of Medicine,* vol. 319 (November 24, 1988), pp. 1392–97.

16. Stephen Litvak and others, "Early Discharge of the Postmastectomy Patient: Unbundling of Hospital Services to Improve Profitability under DRGs," *American Surgeon,* vol. 53 (October 1987), pp. 577–79.

17. HCFA, *1985 Impact Report,* Pub. 03251, chap. 4; and Viola B. Latta and Charles Helbing, "Medicare: Short-Stay Hospital Services, by Leading Diagnosis-Related Groups, 1983 and 1985," *Health Care Financing Review,* vol. 10 (Winter 1988), pp. 79–107, esp. pp. 79–80, 86–88.

18. Louise B. Russell and Jane E. Sisk, "Medical Technology in the United

States: The Last Decade," *International Journal of Technology Assessment in Health Care,* vol. 4, no. 2 (1988), p. 276.

19. General Accounting Office, *Medicare: Past Overuse of Intensive Care Services Inflates Hospital Payments,* GAO/HRD-86-25 (March 1986); DesHarnais and others, "Early Effects of the Prospective Payment System"; and DesHarnais and others, "Impact of the Prospective Payment System."

20. GAO, *Medicare: Past Overuse of Intensive Care,* pp. 22–23.

21. DesHarnais and others, "Early Effects of the Prospective Payment System"; and DesHarnais and others, "Impact of the Prospective Payment System."

22. Frank A. Sloan, Michael A. Morrisey, and Joseph Valvona, "Medicare Prospective Payment and the Use of Medical Technologies in Hospitals," *Medical Care,* vol. 26 (September 1988), pp. 837–53.

23. DesHarnais and others, "Early Effects of the Prospective Payment System," p. 10.

24. DesHarnais and others, "Impact of the Prospective Payment System," p. 5.

25. Michael J. Long and others, "The Effect of PPS on Hospital Product and Productivity," *Medical Care,* vol. 25 (June 1987), pp. 528–38; and Sloan and others, "Medicare Prospective Payment and the Use of Medical Technologies."

26. Long and others, "Effects of PPS on Hospital Product and Productivity."

27. Sloan and others, "Medicare Prospective Payment and the Use of Medical Technologies."

28. Jerry Cromwell and Greg Pope, "The Impact of Medicare's Prospective Payment System on Medical Device Innovation" (Needham, Mass.: Health Economics Research, November 7, 1988), p. 7; and ProPAC, *Medicare Prospective Payment and the American Health Care System: Report to Congress* (Washington, June 1988), p. 37.

29. DesHarnais and others, "Early Effects of the Prospective Payment System"; and DesHarnais and others, "Impact of the Prospective Payment System."

30. HCFA, "Medicare Data: Participating Facilities, 1967–86," Department of Health and Human Services, unpublished tables, n.d.

31. HCFA, *1985 Impact Report,* Pub. 03251, p. 6.25a.

32. Division of National Cost Estimates, Office of the Actuary, HCFA, "National Health Expenditures, 1986–2000," *Health Care Financing Review,* vol. 8 (Summer 1987), table 18. These are nursing home expenditures for patients of all ages, but the percentages given for the elderly in the last article on expenditures by age-group are similar. See Charles R. Fisher, "Differences by Age Groups in Health Care Spending," *Health Care Financing Review,* vol. 1 (Spring 1980), p. 89.

33. National Association for Home Care, "A Profile of the Home Care

Community: Basic Statistics on Home Care," Home Care Fact Sheet 1 (Winter–Spring, 1988).

34. Yvonne M. Lyles, "Impact of Medicare Diagnosis-Related Groups (DRGs) on Nursing Homes in the Portland, Oregon Metropolitan Area," *Journal of the American Geriatrics Society,* vol. 34 (August 1986), pp. 573–78; David Klingman and others, "The Impact of Medicare Prospective Payment on Medicaid-Funded Post-Hospital Care: Executive Summary from the Draft Final Report" (SysteMetrics/McGraw-Hill, May 15, 1987); and Carolyne Davis, "Assessing Medicare's Prospective Payment System," *Journal of the American Medical Association,* vol. 257 (April 3, 1987), pp. 1793–94.

35. Judith Feder, William Scanlon, and Jody Hoffman, "Spillovers from Medicare PPS: Preliminary Results from a Nursing Home Survey," paper presented at the October 1987 meeting of the American Public Health Association.

36. Lyles, "Impact of Medicare Diagnosis-Related Groups."

37. Mark A. Sager, Elaine A. Leventhal, and Douglas V. Easterling, "The Impact of the Medicare Prospective Payment System on Wisconsin Nursing Homes," *Journal of the American Medical Association,* vol. 257 (April 3, 1987), pp. 1762–66.

38. Mark A. Sager and others, "Changes in the Location of Death after Passage of Medicare's Prospective Payment System: A National Study," *New England Journal of Medicine,* vol. 320 (February 16, 1989), pp. 433–39.

39. Mary Ann Lewis and others, "The Initial Effects of the Prospective Payment System on Nursing Home Patients," *American Journal of Public Health,* vol. 77 (July 1987), pp. 819–21.

40. Lewis and others, "Initial Effects of the Prospective Payment System," p. 821.

41. Norman V. Carroll and W. Gary Erwin, "Patient Shifting as a Response to Medicare Prospective Payment," *Medical Care,* vol. 25 (December 1987), pp. 1161–67.

42. C. R. Neu and Scott C. Harrison, "Posthospital Care before and after the Medicare Prospective Payment System," paper presented at the October 1987 meeting of the American Public Health Association; and C. R. Neu and Scott C. Harrison, *Posthospital Care before and after the Medicare Prospective Payment System,* Report R-3590-HCFA (Santa Monica, Calif.: Rand Corp., March 1988).

43. Two other studies deserve mention. The University of Colorado's Center for Health Services Research looked at changes in the types of patients cared for by nursing homes in six states before and under prospective payment. Researchers examined homes with high and low percentages of medicare-covered days separately. In a brief, qualitative description of the findings, the *1986 Impact Report* states that, in the high-percentage homes, the number of patients with "subacute" problems, that is, problems suggesting recovery from an acute condition, increased substantially between 1983

and 1986. See HCFA, *Report to Congress: The Impact of the Medicare Hospital Prospective Payment System, 1986 Annual Report,* Pub. 03281 (Baltimore: Department of Health and Human Services, June 1989), pp. 7.16–7.18. This may be one reason that patients with chronic conditions appear to be increasingly diverted to more traditional nursing homes, which do not specialize in the care of subacute cases.

The other study reviewed patients at the time they were discharged from the hospital to determine whether they were "sicker," meaning less able to function on their own. See Merilyn Coe, Anne Wilkinson, and Patricia Patterson, "Final Report on the Dependency at Discharge Study" (Beaverton, Ore.: Northwest Oregon Health Systems, May 1986). The study examined all patients in five diagnostic groups who were discharged from four Portland hospitals, regardless of where they went after the hospital. Measured in terms of a scale based on their ability to walk and bathe themselves, their symptoms, and the procedures required for their care, the authors found that patients discharged in 1984/5 were more dependent than those discharged in 1981/3. The study did not, however, make any adjustments for the changes in coding induced by prospective payment, so it is likely that, although they were classified in the same DRGs, the patients were not comparable in the two years. Further, as any study of its kind would have been, this study was subject to problems caused by the decline in admissions—the average severity of patients could indeed have increased, even if they were no sicker than before, simply because the least sick were no longer being admitted to hospitals at all. The omission of stays over 22 days may also have left out the most seriously ill patients in the earlier period, when stays were longer, thus biasing the severity measure for the earlier year. The DRGs included in the study were stroke, pneumonia, heart failure, hip replacement, and major joint pinning.

44. Sandy Lutz, "Home Health Denial Prompting Mergers, Reductions in Services to Medicare Patients," *Modern Healthcare,* vol. 17 (November 6, 1987), pp. 119, 122; and House Select Committee on Aging, "Pepper Releases CBO Analysis Documenting $2.4 Billion Cut in Federal Spending on Long-Term Care for the Elderly; Cites Administration's 'Blatant Disregard for the Elderly's Needs,'" *News,* February 5, 1988.

45. Charles R. Fisher, "Physician Charges for Surgical Services under Medicare, by Medical Specialty: 1980 and 1985," *Health Care Financing Review,* vol. 9 (Summer 1988), pp. 127–32.

46. Thomas F. Imperiale and others, "Preadmission Screening of Medicare Patients: The Clinical Impact of Reimbursement Disapproval," *Journal of the American Medical Association,* vol. 259 (June 17, 1988), pp. 3418–21.

47. That technological change permitted but did not cause the shift to outpatient cataract surgery is suggested by the fact that, in 1982, it was still the case that only about 10 percent of these procedures were done in outpatient settings. Over the preceding 15 years, because of the increasing ease and safety of the surgery, the length of stay for inpatient procedures dropped from 7.6 days, in 1966, to 3.2 days in 1981. See Louis P. Garrison and Sandra M.

Yamashiro, "Background Paper on Cataract Surgery and Physician Payment under the Medicare Program," prepared for the Health Program, Office of Technology Assessment, U.S. Congress, October 1985, pp. 1-2, 3-7. See also Office of Technology Assessment, *Appropriate Care for Cataract Surgery Patients before and after Surgery: Issues of Medical Safety and Appropriateness* (October 1988), p. 19.

48. Michele Robinson, "Part B Costs: Outpatient Spending Fuels Surge," *Hospitals* (November 5, 1987), p. 27.

49. Ronald J. Lagoe and John W. Milliren, "A Community-Based Analysis of Ambulatory Surgery Utilization," *American Journal of Public Health,* vol. 76 (February 1986), pp. 150–53.

50. Mark F. Baldwin, "Hospitals Wary of Impact of Reforms in Medicare Outpatient Surgery Pay," *Modern Healthcare,* vol. 16 (December 5, 1986), pp. 22, 24.

51. Sandy Lutz, "Outpatient Surgery Centers Slated for Growth as Fees, Demand Increase," *Modern Healthcare,* vol. 17 (January 16, 1987), p. 54.

52. DesHarnais and others, "Impact of the Prospective Payment System."

53. Brenda Marshall, Susan DesHarnais, and James Chesney, "Ambulatory Surgery Trends: Implications for Hospitals," paper presented at the October 1987 meeting of the American Public Health Association.

54. Baldwin, "Hospitals Wary of Impact"; Office of Inspector General, *Utilization and Quality Control . . . (PRO) Program: Quality Review Activities.*

Chapter Four

1. *Quality of Care under Medicare's Prospective Payment System,* Hearings before the Senate Special Committee on Aging, September 26, October 24, and November 12, 1985, 99 Cong. 1 sess., serial 99-9, 10, 11, vol. 1 (Government Printing Office, 1985), p. 1.

2. Regression analyses of the death rate for all people aged 65 or older (see Health Care Financing Administration, Office of Research and Demonstrations, *Report to Congress: Impact of the Medicare Hospital Prospective Payment System, 1985 Annual Report,* HCFA Pub. 03251 [Baltimore: U.S. Department of Health and Human Services, August 1987], pp. 4.52–4.54), and of death rates for five-year age-groups for men and women separately (by the author and not presented here), also show the strongest results for a break in trend in 1979, not later. The purpose of the regressions for the detailed age-sex groups was to determine whether all groups appeared to follow a similar trend, or whether some, particularly the most vulnerable, the very old, showed clearer effects of prospective payment than the rest. For each group, data for the period 1970–85 were tested for a break in trend in 1979, 1982, and 1983. The break in 1979 was significant for the largest number of groups. The regressions provided no evidence of any difference in effects among the groups;

in particular, the breaks in 1982 and 1983 were not statistically significant for men or women aged 85 and older.

3. Yvonne M. Lyles, "Impact of Medicare Diagnosis-Related Groups (DRGs) on Nursing Homes in the Portland, Oregon Metropolitan Area," *Journal of the American Geriatrics Society*, vol. 34 (August 1986), pp. 573–78; Mark A. Sager, Elaine A. Leventhal, and Douglas V. Easterling, "The Impact of Medicare's Prospective Payment System on Wisconsin Nursing Homes," *Journal of the American Medical Association*, vol. 257 (April 3, 1987), pp. 1762–66; and Mark A. Sager and others, "Changes in the Location of Death after Passage of Medicare's Prospective Payment System: A National Study," *New England Journal of Medicine*, vol. 320 (February 16, 1989), pp. 433–39.

4. Susan DesHarnais and others, "The Early Effects of the Prospective Payment System on Inpatient Utilization and the Quality of Care," *Inquiry*, vol. 24 (Spring 1987), pp. 7–16; and Susan DesHarnais, James Chesney, and Steven Fleming, "The Impact of the Prospective Payment System on Hospital Utilization and the Quality of Care: Trends and Regional Variations in the First Two Years," paper presented at the October 1987 meeting of the American Public Health Association.

5. HCFA, *1985 Impact Report*, Pub. 03251, p. 4.43.

6. *Quality of Care*, Hearings, vol. 1.

7. "Are DRGs Effective?" *Washington Report on Medicine and Health*, vol. 38 (May 7, 1984).

8. Office of Inspector General, Office of Analysis and Inspections, *National DRG Validation Study: Special Report on Premature Discharges*, OAI-05-88-00740 (Washington: Department of Health and Human Services, February 1988), pp. i–ii.

9. Office of Inspector General, Office of Analysis and Inspections, *Utilization and Quality Control Peer Review Organization (PRO) Program: Quality Review Activities*, OAI-01-88-00570 (Washington: Department of Health and Human Services, August 1988), pp. 3–4.

10. HCFA, *1985 Impact Report*, Pub. 03251, p. 3.19.

11. DesHarnais and others, "Early Effects of the Prospective Payment System."

12. Frank A. Sloan, Michael A. Morrisey, and Joseph Valvona, "Case Shifting and the Medicare Prospective Payment System," *American Journal of Public Health*, vol. 78 (May 1988), pp. 553–56.

13. HCFA, *Report to Congress: The Impact of the Medicare Hospital Prospective Payment System, 1986 Annual Report*, Pub. 03281 (Baltimore: Department of Health and Human Services, June 1989), p. 4.7a.

14. The appearance of a number of studies that claim to be able to identify high-cost patients on the basis of information available before admission indicates that it is important to continue to monitor for the possibility of problems in special groups. See, for example, Eric Munoz and others, "Hospital

Costs, Resource Characteristics, and the Dynamics of Death for Patients with Hypertension," *Archives of Internal Medicine,* vol. 148 (August 1988), pp. 1729–32; and Randall S. Vollertsen and others, "Economic Outcome under Medicare Prospective Payment at a Tertiary-Care Institution: The Effects of Demographic, Clinical, and Logistic Factors on Duration of Hospital Stay and Part A Charges for Medical Back Problems (DRG 243)," *Mayo Clinic Proceedings,* vol. 63 (1988), pp. 583–91.

15. Thomas G. Dehn, "Less Profit, Less Care? Reassessing the Impact of Medicare and Medicaid Costs," testimony before the House Select Committee on Aging, February 16, 1988, p. 1.

16. William L. Roper and Glenn M. Hackbarth, "HCFA's Agenda for Promoting High-Quality Care," *Health Affairs,* special issue on the Pursuit of Quality, vol. 7 (Spring 1988), pp. 91–98.

17. R. Heather Palmer, "The Challenges and Prospects for Quality Assessment and Assurance in Ambulatory Care," *Inquiry,* vol. 25 (Spring 1988), pp. 119–31.

18. John F. Fitzgerald and others, "Changing Patterns of Hip Fracture Care before and after Implementation of the Prospective Payment System," *Journal of the American Medical Association,* vol. 258 (July 10, 1987), pp. 218–21; and John F. Fitzgerald, Patricia S. Moore, and Robert S. Dittus, "The Care of Elderly Patients with Hip Fracture: Changes since Implementation of the Prospective Payment System," *New England Journal of Medicine,* vol. 319 (November 24, 1988), pp. 1392–97.

19. A major study that appears to be of this sort has been undertaken by the Rand Corporation with funds from the Health Care Financing Administration. Using a sample of 17,000 medical records, the project will compare the hospital care given to patients in six diagnostic groups—hip fracture is one—before and after the introduction of prospective payment. See Paul W. Eggers, "Prospective Payment System and Quality: Early Results and Research Strategy," *Health Care Financing Review, 1987 Annual Supplement* (1987), pp. 29–37. The study will not be able to track the patients' care after they leave the hospital.

20. Allen Dobson, "The Impact on the U.S. Health Care System," in Paul C. Rettig and others, "Symposium Report: Medicare's Prospective Payment System—The Expectations and the Realities," *Inquiry,* vol. 24 (Summer 1987), p. 180.

21. Office of Inspector General, *Utilization and Quality Control . . . (PRO) Program: Quality Review Activities,* pp. 2–4.

22. Peter E. Dans, Jonathan P. Weiner, and Sharon E. Otter, "Peer Review Organizations: Promises and Potential Pitfalls," *New England Journal of Medicine,* vol. 313 (October 31, 1985), pp. 1131–37; Sharon McIlrath, "PRO Contract Negotiations Under Way Soon," *American Medical News* (March 11, 1988), pp. 2, 35; and Office of Inspector General, *Utilization and Quality Control . . . (PRO) Program: Quality Review Activities.*

23. Dans and others, "Peer Review Organizations"; and Mohammad N. Akhter, "PRO Review of Hospital Admissions of Medicare Patients," *Missouri Medicine,* vol. 82 (March 1985), p. 126.

24. Physician Payment Review Commission, *Annual Report to Congress, 1988* (Washington, March 31, 1988), p. 196.

25. Office of Inspector General, *Utilization and Quality Control ... (PRO) Program: Quality Review Activities,* p. 3; Frederic R. Curtiss, "Final Regulations on Medicare Prospective Pricing," *American Journal of Hospital Pharmacy,* vol. 41 (April 1984), pp. 716–20; and Mark F. Baldwin, "Hospitals Face Tougher PRO Reviews," *Modern Healthcare,* vol. 16 (January 31, 1986), p. 16.

26. Office of Inspector General, *Utilization and Quality Control ... (PRO) Program: Quality Review Activities,* pp. 3–5.

27. HCFA, Office of Medical Review, Health Standards and Quality Bureau, "Generic Quality Screens" (Baltimore: Department of Health and Human Services, n.d.).

28. Office of Inspector General, *Utilization and Quality Control ... (PRO) Program: Quality Review Activities,* pp. 6–8.

29. Sharon McIlrath, "AMA Fights PRO Sanction Process," *American Medical News* (April 24, 1987), pp. 1, 50; and Office of Inspector General, *Utilization and Quality Control ... (PRO) Program: Quality Review Activities,* pp. 7–10.

30. Office of Inspector General, *Utilization and Quality Control ... (PRO) Program: Quality Review Activities,* pp. 12–13.

31. Office of Inspector General, Office of Analysis and Inspections, *National DRG Validation Study: Quality of Patient Care in Hospitals,* OAI-09-88-00870 (Washington: Department of Health and Human Services, July 1989), pp. 2, 5; and Health Data Institute, *National DRG Validation Study,* report prepared for the Office of Inspector General, Department of Health and Human Services (Lexington, Mass., November 1987).

32. "Briefly This Week," *McGraw-Hill's Medicine and Health,* vol. 43 (February 6, 1989), p. 4.

33. Spencer Vibbert, "Quality Data: How Good Is It?" *McGraw-Hill's Medicine and Health,* vol. 43 (January 23, 1989), p. 1.

34. HCFA, *Medicare Hospital Mortality Information, 1987,* Pub. 00642 (Baltimore: Department of Health and Human Services, December 1988), vols. 1–14, p. v.

35. HCFA, *Medicare Hospital Mortality Information,* pp. vi, vii.

36. Department of Health and Human Services, *HHS News,* December 15, 1988, p. 2.

37. Dehn, "Less Profit, Less Care?"; and P.L. 99-509, sec. 9353.

38. Palmer, "Challenges and Prospects"; HCFA, "Quality of Care Review of Services Provided by Risk Sharing Health Maintenance Organizations (HMOs) and Competitive Medical Plans (CMPs): Exhibit C.1, Scope of Work," RFP HCFA 87-018 (Baltimore: Department of Health and Human

Services, March 1987); Office of Inspector General, *Utilization and Quality Control . . . (PRO) Program: Quality Review Activities,* pp. 22–23; and Harris Meyer, "PROs Plot Review of Medicare HMO Care," *American Medical News* (August 14, 1987), pp. 2, 43.

39. Robert Pear, "U.S. to Let Consumers See Medicare Data on Health Care Quality," *New York Times,* April 16, 1985, p. B20.

40. During the first round (1984–86), $322.4 million was spent on PRO contracts; $446.2 million was budgeted for the second round (1986–88). The second-round contracts will be extended in order to stagger contract negotiations for the third round, and during the extension the Health Care Financing Administration expects to spend $183.3 million. The third round, which brings an increased workload and adds one more year to the contract period, is estimated to cost about $1,019 million. Data supplied by Health Care Financing Administration.

41. Donald M. Berwick, "Sounding Board: Continuous Improvement as an Ideal in Health Care," *New England Journal of Medicine,* vol. 320 (January 5, 1989), pp. 53–56.

42. Robert W. Haley and others, "The Financial Incentive for Hospitals to Prevent Nosocomial Infections under the Prospective Payment System: An Empirical Determination from a Nationally Representative Sample," *Journal of the American Medical Association,* vol. 257 (March 27, 1987), pp. 1611–14.

43. Paul Ginsburg, "Commentary," in Rettig and others, "Symposium Report," p. 187.

44. HCFA, *1985 Impact Report,* Pub. 03251, pp. 4.2–4.3.

45. "Statement of Nancy M. Gordon, Assistant Director, Human Resources and Community Development Division, before Subcommittee on Health, Senate Finance Committee, April 7, 1987," Congressional Budget Office, p. 2.

46. Roper and Hackbarth, "HCFA's Agenda," p. 96.

47. Physician Payment Review Commission, *Annual Report, 1988,* p. 190.

48. David M. Eddy and John Billings, "The Quality of Medical Evidence: Implications for Quality of Care," *Health Affairs,* special issue on the Pursuit of Quality, vol. 7 (Spring 1988), p. 20.

49. Kathleen N. Lohr, Karl D. Yordy, and Samuel O. Thier, "Current Issues in Quality of Care," *Health Affairs,* special issue on the Pursuit of Quality, vol. 7 (Spring 1988), p. 10.

Chapter Five

1. Inpatient hospital care accounts for 93 percent of the outlays of the Hospital Insurance Trust Fund. See *1987 Annual Report of the Board of Trustees of the Federal Hospital Insurance Trust Fund* (Washington: U.S. Department of Health and Human Services, 1987), p. 57.

2. Annual reports of the Trustees of the Federal Hospital Insurance Trust Fund, 1979–88. These annual reports, as well as those by the Trustees of the Federal Supplementary Medical Insurance Trust Fund, are initially printed by the U.S. Department of Health and Human Services and subsequently reprinted by the Congress.

3. *1980 Annual Report, Federal Hospital Insurance Trust Fund*, H. Doc. 96-333, 96 Cong. 2 sess. (Government Printing Office, 1980), pp. 26, 31.

4. Michele Robinson, "Part B Costs: Outpatient Spending Fuels Surge," *Hospitals* (November 5, 1987), p. 27.

5. *1988 Annual Report of the Board of Trustees of the Federal Supplementary Medical Insurance Trust Fund* (Washington: Department of Health and Human Services, 1988), p. 6.

6. *1987 Annual Report of the Board of Trustees of the Federal Supplementary Medical Insurance Trust Fund* (Washington: Department of Health and Human Services, 1987), pp. 6, 29, table 5.

7. The trustees of the Supplementary Medical Insurance Trust Fund only project expenditures for the current year (which is not over at the time their report is published) and two future years. Thus 1990 is the last year for which projections are available in the 1988 report. The rationale for the different treatment of the two trust funds arises from their different methods of financing: the Hospital Insurance Trust Fund is financed by a special tax that can only be changed by new legislation, while the Supplementary Medical Insurance Trust Fund is financed by a combination of enrollee premiums, which are changed automatically every year, and general federal tax revenues.

8. *1988 Annual Report of the Board of Trustees of the Federal Hospital Insurance Trust Fund* (Washington: Department of Health and Human Services, 1988), p. 13.

9. Health Care Financing Administration, Office of Research and Demonstrations, *Report to Congress: Impact of the Medicare Hospital Prospective Payment System, 1985 Annual Report*, HCFA Pub. 03251 (Baltimore: U.S. Department of Health and Human Services, 1987), pp. 4.76–4.78.

10. Prospective Payment Assessment Commission (ProPAC), *Medicare Prospective Payment and the American Health Care System: Report to the Congress* (Washington, June 1988), p. 79. Numbers for 1989 are from the Congressional Budget Office. Besides the basic Part B premium, enrollees began paying a premium to help pay for the new catastrophic insurance program in 1989 ($48 a year for 1989).

11. ProPAC, *Medicare Prospective Payment* (1988), chap. 4; and HCFA, *1985 Impact Report*, Pub. 03251, chap. 4.

12. "Congress Clears Catastrophic Insurance," *McGraw-Hill's Medicine and Health*, vol. 42 (June 13, 1988), p. 1.

13. Joyce Freiden, "Catastrophic Bill: Good News, Bad News for Providers," *McGraw-Hill's Medicine and Health*, vol. 42 (December 19, 1988).

14. Richard M. Scheffler, James O. Gibbs, and Dolores A. Gurnick, "The Impact of Medicare's Prospective Payment System and Private Sector Initia-

tives: Blue Cross Experience, 1980–1986," report prepared by the Blue Cross and Blue Shield Association with the Research Program in Health Economics, University of California, Berkeley, under HCFA grant 15-C-98757/5-01 (July 1988).

15. Frank A. Sloan, Michael A. Morrisey, and Joseph Valvona, "Effects of the Medicare Prospective Payment System on Hospital Cost Containment: An Early Appraisal," *Milbank Quarterly,* vol. 66 (1988), pp. 191–220.

16. See ProPAC, *Medicare Prospective Payment* (1988), p. 91. The commission notes, however, that medical expenditures are still growing faster than the gross national product, and thus it appears that medical care will continue to increase its share of the nation's resources.

17. ProPAC, *Medicare Prospective Payment* (1988), chaps. 2–3; and Office of Inspector General, "OIG Audit Report—Preliminary Analysis of Hospital Profit Margins in the Third Year of the Prospective Payment System—CIN: A-07-87-00051," memo to William L. Roper, HCFA administrator (Washington: Department of Health and Human Services, January 25, 1988).

18. ProPAC, *Medicare Prospective Payment* (1988), p. 45.

19. "Statement of Jack W. Owen, Executive Vice President, American Hospital Association, Washington, D.C.," in *Hospital Profits under the Prospective Payment System,* Hearing before the Subcommittee on Health of the Senate Finance Committee, February 21, 1986, 99 Cong. 2 sess (GPO, 1986), pp. 82–84.

20. ProPAC, *Medicare Prospective Payment* (1988), p. 45.

21. ProPAC, *Medicare Prospective Payment* (1988), p. 47; and "OIG Audit Report," p. 4.

22. ProPAC, *Medicare Prospective Payment* (1988), chap. 2; and "OIG Audit Report."

23. The two major studies base their calculations on different samples of hospitals. The Prospective Payment Assessment Commission studied the cost reports of 2,862 hospitals, while the inspector general of the Department of Health and Human Services studied a scientifically selected sample of about 240 hospitals (expanded to 254 in PPS-3). Their profit estimates were very close for the first two years, but diverged in 1986, the Prospective Payment Assessment Commission estimating 8.2 percent, the inspector general 9.6 percent. ProPAC, *Medicare Prospective Payment* (1988), p. 47, tables 2-8, 2-9; and "OIG Audit Report," p. 4.

24. "Profit Margin Data Agitate Industry," *Hospitals* (February 20, 1987), pp. 22–24; and "OIG Audit Report."

25. ProPAC, *Medicare Prospective Payment* (1988), p. 47, table 2-8.

26. Judith Feder, Jack Hadley, and Stephen Zuckerman, "How Did Medicare's Prospective Payment System Affect Hospitals?" *New England Journal of Medicine,* vol. 317 (October 1, 1987), pp. 867–73.

27. ProPAC, *Medicare Prospective Payment* (1988), p. 47, table 2-8.

28. Office of Inspector General, "Causes of Profits Earned by Hospitals Subject to the Prospective Payment System—CIN: A-14-87-00104," memo to

William L. Roper, HCFA administrator (Washington: Department of Health and Human Services, April 6, 1987).

29. ProPAC, *Medicare Prospective Payment* (1988), pp. 61–63; and ProPAC, *Report and Recommendations to the Secretary, U.S. Department of Health and Human Services, 1989* (Washington, March 1, 1989), p. 14.

30. ProPAC, "PPS Costs, Revenue, and Margins: Preliminary Estimates, December 1988," memo, Washington, December 14, 1988.

31. Owen testimony before Senate Subcommittee on Health; and ProPAC, *Medicare Prospective Payment* (1988), chap. 2.

32. Richard P. Kusserow, inspector general, Department of Health and Human Services, "Statement before the Health Task Force of the House Budget Committee on Medicare Hospital Profits," August 1, 1988; and ProPAC, "PPS Costs, Revenue, and Margins."

33. ProPAC, *Medicare Prospective Payment* (1988), chap. 3.

34. "OIG Audit Report"; and Kusserow, "Statement before the Health Task Force."

35. Carol M. McCarthy, "DRGs—Five Years Later," *New England Journal of Medicine,* vol. 318 (June 23, 1988), pp. 1683–86.

36. Allen Dobson and Elizabeth W. Hoy, "Hospital PPS Profits: Past and Prospective," *Health Affairs,* special issue on the Pursuit of Quality (Spring 1988), pp. 126–29.

Chapter Six

1. Frank A. Sloan, Michael A. Morrisey, and Joseph Valvona, "Case Shifting and the Medicare Prospective Payment System," *American Journal of Public Health,* vol. 78 (May 1988), pp. 553–56.

2. John F. Fitzgerald and others, "Changing Patterns of Hip Fracture Care before and after Implementation of the Prospective Payment System," *Journal of the American Medical Association,* vol. 258 (July 10, 1987), pp. 218–21; and John F. Fitzgerald, Patricia S. Moore, and Robert S. Dittus, "The Care of Elderly Patients with Hip Fracture: Changes since Implementation of the Prospective Payment System," *New England Journal of Medicine,* vol. 319 (November 24, 1988), pp. 1392–97.

3. R. Heather Palmer, "The Challenges and Prospects for Quality Assessment and Assurance in Ambulatory Care," *Inquiry,* vol. 25 (Spring 1988), pp. 119–31.

4. William L. Roper and Glenn M. Hackbarth, "Commentary: HCFA's Agenda for Promoting High-Quality Care," *Health Affairs,* special issue on the Pursuit of Quality, vol. 7 (Spring 1988), pp. 91–98; and Health Care Financing Administration, Office of Research and Demonstrations, *Report to Congress: Impact of the Medicare Hospital Prospective Payment System, 1985 Annual Report,* HCFA Pub. 03251 (Baltimore: U.S. Department of Health and Human Services, August 1987), pp. 1.10–1.11.

5. "HCFA to Put Its Data to Work in Measuring Medical Effectiveness," *McGraw-Hill's Medicine and Health,* vol. 42 (June 20, 1988), p. 1.

6. Carol M. McCarthy, "DRGs—Five Years Later," *New England Journal of Medicine,* vol. 318 (June 23, 1988), pp. 1683–86.

7. Judith Feder, Jack Hadley, and Stephen Zuckerman, "How Did Medicare's Prospective Payment System Affect Hospitals?" *New England Journal of Medicine,* vol. 317 (October 1, 1987), pp. 867–73; and Judith Feder, Jack Hadley, and Stephen Zuckerman, "Setting a Fairer Price for Medicare," *Washington Post* editorial, May 3, 1988, p. A22. This proposal resembles the state rate-setting system in New Jersey, which uses DRGs and develops rates from a blend of the hospital's costs and the costs of similar hospitals. See William C. Hsiao and others, "Lessons of the New Jersey DRG Payment System," *Health Affairs,* vol. 5 (Summer 1986), pp. 32–45.

8. Prospective Payment Assessment Commission, *Medicare Prospective Payment and the American Health Care System: Report to the Congress* (Washington, June 1988), pp. 6–7.

INDEX